CONTENTS

Part Three

Part Four

Introduction

The present book has a complex nature just like its subject matter, natural language. My approach to natural language as an information state reflects inherent complexity and this is precisely the reason why the theoretical framework I have been progressively developing has resulted in a highly articulated and complex one.

The present book consists of four parts: the first presents the theoretical background of both my CPP-TRS Theory of Text Comprehension and CPP-TRS Theory of Text Compression as well as the range of phenomena that are being handled.

The second part presents the new implications, the progressive shifts and the radical changes in viewing and rethinking of language within a CPP-TRS perspective, as well as the new terminology I have introduced and the main concepts I have redefined to make sure there is no ambiguity or misunderstanding about already existing terms.

The third part presents in a more detailed way the CPP-TRS Language and Methodology; it has been my very specific intention to familiarize the reader with the highly articulated visual system on which CPP-TRS is based for interpretation of qualitatively different components in natural language.

The fourth part presents those applications that I have personally designed up to the present time and provides some information about those future developments that can be foreseen. As in the analysis of physical matter, many levels of observation may legitimately be adopted in order to focus on different aspects both at a macroscopic and at a microscopic level. In the same way I introduce new tools for observing, describing and explaining qualitatively different phenomena in natural language.

I then proceed towards the organization of a theoretical framework based on a new way of viewing language in terms of a Quantum Linguistics based on quantitative and qualitative reasoning about communication "via natural language".

The present book can also be seen as a kind of systematic and scientifically based justification of the CPP-TRS framework for an audience that has never been exposed to it.

It has been only by a complex path that I have been able to come up with a system of interpretation that works as a language by itself and which can be applied at different levels to any communicative situation, by following precise rules based both on a highly consensual agreement and on a personalized way of adapting the system to a wide variety of cases with no contradiction between the apparently conflicting attitudes considered.

The present book is intended for a diverse audience. I have two types of readers in mind: a) the reader who already knows something about CPP-TRS theory by having read my earlier papers and books and b) the reader who knows nothing about CPP-TRS.

For these two groups, I have thus had to take care in the way the information is provided so that the reader can avoid meeting terminology without knowing that he will find it thoroughly explained somewhere in the book. For this reason I have inserted reading instructions that propose different navigation paths within the book, depending on which group the reader identifies himself with.

There is another distinction or set of distinctions I have made about the intent of each part of the book and about the different attitudes each part intends to trigger.

In the first part the reader finds statements and assertions but not much explanation, and terms are taken for granted, leaving the reader with many unanswered questions.

In the second part I explore the new terms and the implications of the new framework analytically. Terms are defined and explained so that the questions raised in the first part are answered.

In the third part I explain CPP-TRS in different ways to different audiences in different chapters. I address the issue of explaining what CPP-TRS is to a strictly linguistic audience first, then to an AI and Virtual Reality audience, to a Cognitive Science audience, to an Operational Research audience, to an Information Design audience and finally to an Internet audience.

There may be some overlap, but my purpose is to promote some learning skills of CPP-TRS and we all know that a learning process will certainly gain from some repetition. Thus if the third section seems repetitive, this is because this was explicitly intended.

The reader may, of course, skip some parts if he/she is convinced that he/she knows enough already. However, I would like to recommend that the reader keep going rather than skip what may look familiar; each chapter adds something new and provides more specific information.

In the fourth part some of the major applications I have designed are introduced. In order to explore each of them, I use specific tools and books. This final section thus turns out to be merely an entrance into a new world.

Thus the present book is complex but not at all confused or random. It is a multilayered text and it may leave the reader with many choices to make according to what he/she actually expects to get out of this book.

Reading Suggestions

The present book follows a whole set of books and papers on different parts of CPP-TRS, which I have already written and published.

Readers already familiar with CPP-TRS may read the present book by following the progressive order of the different parts.

Readers who have not previously been exposed to CPP-TRS are recommended to start with the third part, and then go back to parts one, two and four so as to be exposed to the different components of CPP-TRS and to be able to understand the theoretical argumentation provided.

One more suggestion: if you want to get the essence of CPP-TRS very quickly go directly to the fourth part. This is specifically intended for journalists, those who need to get some information immediately ... and correctly!

The author trusts readers will forgive her for the frequent repetition of her name and that they will get the right impression about her writing several chapters in the first person, an unusual occurence in science papers or books. The reason why this has been done is to show the struggling and progressive discovery which evolved in her personal experience and full life.

Of course, this may sound 'self-centred', but by reversing the coin it is possible to see that by doing it so explicitly, she is also taking the full responsibility for what she experienced first, designed and tested later, and finally wrote including the supporting evidence for her strong assertions.

Part One

Introduction to CPP-TRS Theory of Text Comprehension and CPP-TRS Theory of Text Compression

Foreword

This book presents a new theoretical framework of qualitative reasoning about communication, which is required in order to understand the need for any working system in natural language processing to be grounded on a consistent and scientifically based model.

CPP-TRS, Communicative Positioning Program and Text Representation Systems, is a visual language based on a highly articulated Theory of Text Comprehension (Tonfoni, 1989-94) and a related Theory of Text Compression (Tonfoni, 1995).

Based on a system of 12 canvases, 10 signs, 14 symbols and a wide set of visual dynamic schemes, CPP-TRS is capable of representing communicative functions, intentions and turn-taking visually. This framework of qualitative reasoning is concerned with aspects of communication which we shall define as qualitative aspects of communication and information via natural language.

In order to identify all these aspects, I have tried to construct a scientific framework that can handle precise facts of language that need a systematic theory for their explanation, not merely noted or described. Any scientist (in this case a scientist of language) needs to be interested not merely in describing and cataloguing facts but also in creating a consistent theory or set of theories that may explain and justify such facts in various ways. Any philosopher of science (in this case a philosopher of the science of language) not only has to analyze isolated language facts but also to analyze the way those facts have been previously identified and then named by the language scientist, who perceives and chooses specific problems to be solved by creating a consistent interpretation framework.

Empirical and conceptual foundations

A basic task of the science of language is to explain language facts and communicative events taking place "via natural language".

Language facts as well as communicative events may be discovered through observational methods. Listening to a conversation when it occurs naturally and recording it, or reading a text and analyzing it, without trying to influence what is happening is a kind of experiment aimed at confronting occurring events so that some consistent model of interpretation can be created.

Chomsky (1957, 1965) has provided the language scientist with a model that promotes an "ad hoc" experiment to observe language facts by asking for evaluation judgements about the very phenomena that are being addressed.

In my observation model there is no predesigned experimental situation, thus ensuring that the individual under observation is acting totally spontaneously. Nevertheless, there are strong and stable points of reference for observation and evaluation on the part of the observer.

In many cases in science, processes and phenomena that cannot be seen may be discovered by using experimental methods employing special equipment, which enables such processes and phenomena to occur on demand and under specially controlled conditions. 'Special equipment' in my observation procedures is the capacity for self-observation and self-reflection as a condition of the observer to recognize what is happening to the individual under observation so that he can provide a system of reference for identifying and consistently naming observed occurrences. Such capacity is the result of both natural attitudes and a system of reference that allows new definitions and a specific terminology to be used and agreed upon by consensus. Without a strongly based system for interpretation, there can be no observation of relevant facts, just random data collection.

Every science employs its own abstractions, terminology and techniques for interpretation and explanation, which may actually be of very different kinds, whereas conceptual elements are ways to make phenomena intelligible.

In my approach those very techniques that are used to detect instruments for self-observation and self-reflection constitute the specific terminology for interpretation and play an explanatory function at a more abstract and conceptual level. I refer to those interpretive visual tools which I have defined as textual canvases, textual machines, textual signs and textual symbols. My theoretical entities may be turned into an independent system, working on top of any language, with its own and highly consistent syntax.

No doubt some global communicative events occur before others; this is why I have kept the productive distinction between "deep structure processes" and "surface structure phenomena", first introduced by Chomsky (1957) for syntax, and have extended it into a kind of explanatory pragmatics.

Relation of theory to observation

In creating a theory we may distinguish between an empiricist and a rationalist attitude. For empiricists, raw facts of experience are primary, and theoretical principles are accepted only when interpreted as generalizations of empirical data; theoretical entities have to be understood as derived and constructed from empirical experiences and need to be strictly related to them.

For rationalists, the scientist's experience is just a disorganized aggregation until some structure and principles are found. A scientist needs therefore to be very selective in observation. Well designed experiments are viewed as "valuable ways to create phenomena which may be significant" (Encyclopedia Britannica).

My theoretical approach is based on both perspectives: on the one hand, there is actual observation of facts derived from experience, then interpreted so as to be generally valid. On the other hand, there is a consistently structured framework with clearly defined parameters and points of reference.

As any theory requires, there are both empirical foundations and a strong and consistent internal organization, which I have precisely defined, to ensure that the parameters I have chosen are reliable and consistent.

A 'new' framework

One of the basic issues in the philosophy of science is the identification of the different styles of explanation in various sciences at different stages and of different stages in a given science. One main concern is also "recognizing periods of shifts in interpretation of concepts and building up of new concepts" (Encyclopedia Britannica).

My approach has evolved progressively over time and has extended in many directions, with different applications. First, I speculated on direct investigation, creating a theory that could explain and justify facts and events, and generate new processes which could not even be thought and conceived in old terms.

I asked myself what kinds of tasks I wanted my new explanatory framework in the science of language to perform and, consequently, what requests its performance could possibly be asked to satisfy.

What became evident was that I had created a new framework by setting up a consistent environment for observing invisible phenomena and highly abstract processes. I found that I had left entirely that kind of scientific approach to language that resembles research in natural sciences, such as botany or entomology, and had foreseen a sort of physics of language, by identifying basic components of language matter and basic energies and forces, which are always active. Further, I have created new language components with special kinds of transformations, which I call "reactions", and I have made "acceleration" possible in text processing.

I have basically entered a completely new universe, which looks in some ways like a research environment in nuclear physics. Thus I have always been aware of an important distinction between language facts and communicative events and the possibility of recreating and reproducing them both, just as in nuclear physics and nuclear chemistry.

The new framework for analyzing language resulted in something completely new and I found that it could be linked to a wide set of applications in real life communicative environments.

A new way of thinking about language: from texture to text

I can state that I have explored language in a completely new way for the following reasons:

- I have always thought about language through highly specific and consistent metaphors that create a common metalanguage that can be shared by the scientific community, to represent text operations, which are precisely defined actions.
- Thinking of text as the final result of a highly complex and dynamic set of processes necessarily implies that its "structure" must have previously undergone many changes; I therefore define text as the result of a text actualization process, which derives from an overall generating "texture" being modified at different times.
- At the "texture" level, text is still a potential and it is possible to see and predict all the dynamics and changes happening before it is actualized into a real text.
- I have identified those processes and made them tangible and visible by creating observational and interpretative tools such as the textual machines and the textual canvases. I have created a model which derives from mechanics, mechanics being that part of physics that states the specific conditions of movement and equilibrium. In other words, I have captured those

cognitive energies and dynamic processes that we can observe as being active in text, within a mechanical framework.

My theory of language may sound like physics — the study of natural phenomena — or chemistry — the science that analyses the composition and structure of elements and explains transformations. Language may certainly be thought of in these ways, as it requires observation of present communicative action and is subject to transformation. The first is illustrated in my Text Comprehension Theory, the second in my Text Compression Theory.

Text Representation Systems

To explain in a detailed way different communicative functions, intentions and turn-taking within an actualized text, I have made all of these invisible aspects visible by creating a set of various text representation systems: TEXTUAL CANVASES, TEXTUAL MACHINES, TEXTUAL SIGNS, TEXTUAL OBJECTS, COGNITIVE SYMBOLS and TURN-TAKING SYMBOLS.

This part of my theory may be considered as OPTICS, where basic conditions of TEXTUAL VISION and TEXT PERCEPTION are presented and thoroughly explained.

All parts of my theory belong to a global theory of text comprehension. I then go further by creating a consistent model for text compression ensuring high accuracy and high consistency. In February 1995 I went one stage further and presented the CPTRU and CPP-TRS clipsheet, as the result of my CPP-TRS Theory of Text Compression, which is the direct consequence of my CPP-TRS Theory of Text Comprehension (Tonfoni, 1989-94).

This final part of this work may be thought of as a kind of kinetics, as it describes the conditions for a new "movement", which is actually acceleration and transformation of parts of previously compressed texts.

I then went further by considering the possibility of attraction and reaction in CPP-TRS processed information territories. Here my research work sounds like nuclear physics because I have identified different kinds of energies in action as well as the possibility of accelerating CPP-TRS processed texts.

A quantum theory of language

Nothing of the kind has ever existed before. Linguistics has never been concerned with problems of acceleration of text segments, while transformations were considered and defined by Chomsky (1957) as acting on a very different level, the syntactical.

I do not want to diminish Chomsky's contribution to linguistics, nor do I want to ignore Searle's contribution to the study of language. Chomsky created an extremely relevant, "corpuscular theory of language", and Searle (1968) went a long way towards an "undulatory approach to language". As in physics, I propose a third way which complements the earlier ones, just as Max Plank did when he stated that energy is both discrete and complex.

The CPP-TRS theory is a quantum theory of language based on elementary and complex textual units carrying communicative energy of three kinds:

a) communicative function (expressed by global control signs);
b) communicative intention (expressed by local control symbols);
c) communicative turn-taking (expressed by either local or global control turn-taking symbols).

This is CPP-TRS based quantum in linguistics.

Einstein underlined the relevance of Plank's theory in 1905 by suggesting that a quantum could be considered as a "package" of light radiation.

A CPTRU is a package of linguistic information with communicative energy that can either be retained or transformed. It is both an elementary unit and a complex one, just as is the quantum in physics. This avoids the dichotomy between "discrete" and "complex"; CPTRU is both discrete and complex.

There is a fundamental distinction between a CPP-TRS Theory of Comprehension and a CPP-TRS Theory of Compression: even though they both apply to text, they apply at very different levels. The CPP-TRS Theory of Text Comprehension applies to texture, the potential of a text, and is concerned with the possibility of actualizing all of the texture potential into as many texts as possible.The CPP-TRS Theory of Text Compression applies specifically to actualized CPTRU that has already been processed and is concerned with specifying function, intention and turn-taking so as to create possible but highly controlled transformations of communicative energy through the application of very specific "forces".

Both theories are the result of a highly consistent and articulated model of language that can be applied at a macro-level (CPP-TRS Theory of Comprehension) or at a micro-level (CPP-TRS Theory of Compression).

Both theories are strictly linked together: the CPP-TRS Theory of Compression is the result of the CPP-TRS Theory of Comprehension. In other words, a CPTRU is the result of an actualized text that has been processed and consistently represented according to the overall system of signs, symbols and other visual schemes that are part of the CPP-TRS Theory of Comprehension.

No text can be consistently compressed if it is not first understood.

Both theories are based on qualitative reasoning about communication, which I have named the Qualitative Communication Framework.

A qualitative communication framework

In the Qualitative Communication Framework I am largely concerned with identifying, defining and consistently applying qualitative reasoning about the value of communicative actions that manifest themselves through language. In order to state basic concepts of qualitative reasoning about communication via natural language I have created a consistent set of visual representation elements specifically aimed at representing invisible aspects of natural language "by turning them into visible and tangible elements". These would have a consistent definition making them shared and agreed conceptual tools for explaining language phenomena, as in physics, or able to produce new language effects and reactions, as in chemistry.

The possibility of controlling transformations and reactions occurring in CPTRU-organized territories of information opens up incredible opportunities. As with any discovery or invention, it is extremely important to explore such possibilities and give serious attention to them.

My entire theory of language, the applications I have personally designed as well as the information control environment that I have planned are aimed at valuing transparency and effectiveness in communication and information processing by promoting awareness and self-reflection processes by the individual.

The 'user' becomes 'chooser'

Being able to see, identify and name processes occurring in information organization means becoming active protagonists of a crucial aspect of life in the era of information technology. When I design a new CPP-TRS application, I like to point out that I am actually turning "the user" of a certain technology into "a chooser", not only because he/she needs to be free to choose whether to use the new tool or not, but also because he/she will have to be aware and skilled in packaging information consistently. In order to do this, he/she will have to know the implications deriving from the various ways of processing information.

If there is an immediate attitude toward communicating and organizing information — because we do communicate and organize information all the time, whenever we use language— there is also a need to improve the process using higher communicative perception.

To clarify this concept, I will give a very simple example: looking at things and seeing them in a general way is different from looking at things and seeing them with a camera at hand to take a picture. In fact, the important thing is the different way of seeing, not merely the camera.

As a result of looking at things differently and using the camera, we get a picture, that is different from what we thought we could see just using our eyes.

What if a camera was a human eye?

In my CPP-TRS Theory of Text Comprehension I distinguish between texture and text. Texture is the result of an information flow taking place and proceeding naturally, as when we talk and write, listen and read. Text is the result of recognising information patterns, which can only take place if we have raised our communicative perception.

There is a fundamental difference between human sight and seeing through a camera: the human eye sees the picture in its context, whereas the same human eye has to see the same object differently through a camera in order to turn it into a picture, because the context is missing.

This is pretty much the difference that exists between texture and text. Text is like the picture, whereas texture is like sight. The picture has be independent from its visual context, which is missing just as the text has to be independent from its communicative context which is also missing.

Nevertheless both the picture and the text retain the distinctive elements of their own context.

A picture may show differences in distance, perspective, colour reproduction and in movement: all of these differences go back to the basic distinction between human sight and what the camera sees.

In the same way a text shows differences in perspective (communicative function), in colour reproduction (communicative intention) and in distance and movement (communicative turn-taking): these differences go back to the basic distinction between immediate communicative attitudes and natural communicative perception attitudes. Just as there is a precise way of looking at things in order to make use of a camera, in the same way we can see specific text-perception being active while communicating textually.

The CPP-TRS Theory of Text Comprehension supports a text producer with a whole set of techniques and tools to regulate and reproduce texture elements that may be lost in text, very much like a photographer who uses special techniques and tools to reproduce and exaggerate something that would otherwise be lost.

Thus CPP-TRS is a methodology aimed at providing new tools and techniques for text representation: a textual cube may exaggerate a certain fact, just as a fish-eye lens exaggerates certain elements of a scene, that do, in fact, exist.

The textual pentagram

My CPP-TRS Theory of Text Comprehension leads the text producer toward organizing a textual pentagram with a clear and precise system of textual notation as a final result. Textual notation, just like music notation, has a precise value and consists of a set of highly articulated interpretative notes, that are consensually shared.

CPP-TRS is both an integrated methodology for recognizing what is happening on a cognitive level when individuals communicate and a visual language for naming and representing those processes that have been previously recognized and accurately described and defined.

CPP-TRS therefore constitutes a specific system for interpretation, that allows each individual to identify and describe the different kinds of operations that occur in communication.

As such, CPP-TRS may productively be used as a consistent system of instructions for indicating what has happened in producing a certain text, but it may also be used as a reliable device for changing a text according to very specific indications that are perceived and understood because they are naturally based, consistently represented and consensually agreed.

Nuclear energy in text processing

It may sound too strong to claim that I have discovered nuclear energy in language and invented tools that may be used to produce such powerful energy both in communication and in information technology. But it is not at all too strong; it is the truth. The CPP-TRS Theory of Text Comprehension allows X-rayed communication and X-rayed information processing to take place. In other words it allows an individual to see "behind and beyond just words and paragraphs and texts", to see a thing he had never been able to see before, even though it had always been there, because it was invisible, unnamed and therefore unknown.

The CPP-TRS Theory of Text Compression allows communicative energy to be transformed and information reactions to take place in certain circumstances and within specific information processing environments, according to precise communication needs, just as nuclear energy, which was first discovered as a natural phenomenon, can be produced for specific applications in "ad hoc" environments.

Just like a physician who discovers something extremely important and realizes the power and the potential of his/her own discovery, I worked up precise identifications of all the possible applications I could foresee. I have always been deeply convinced that, having created my theories and tested them accurately, it was my duty to use foresight and design the applications so that they would result in something helpful and positive for humanity rather than something extremely powerful controlled arbitrarily by a very limited number of people.

The scientist needs to feel responsible for both theories and applications

A responsible scientist, while making important discoveries, should never forget to pay attention to educational environments. Supporting teaching with experiments will favour experimental reasoning by the student. Textual machines can be thought of as experiments that directly support reasoning about language and communication. The Text Comprehension Theory may be applied to a large set of different domains and can be seen to be very effective.

The Text Compression Theory, which I have derived as a natural consequence of the Text Comprehension Theory, can be used for very precise applications provided they are subject to control.

The matter of controlling CPTRU territories, which are the result of a Text Compression Process, is a very delicate issue. The control within my CPP-TRS framework resides both in the encoding and decoding processes.

CPTRU is a highly compressed information unit, having been derived from a CPP-TRS pre-processed text, which may be retrieved and recognized in its original state.

Any transformation process in my system leaves a trace and this guarantees that one can recognize the kind of operations that have been performed.

I have deliberately followed the same principle of leaving visible what has happened even in text-acceleration when text reactions occur. The crucial matter is where the control and transparency will be active and up to which level. The consistency of the overall process guarantees the whole mechanism, which may be monitored, controlled, checked and made transparent at different levels.

The issue therefore becomes how much communicative competence different individuals involved in the process will gain.

I have personally dedicated so much energy and time to the design of educational applications because I want to promote cognitive awareness by supporting cognitive self-reflection as a reassurance for the individual that he/she can be personally in control of a whole set of information processing activities as well as communicative actions, which derive from the newly designed applications and tools. Self-reflection is a scientifically based process allowing the individual to see and understand what is going on in communication and letting him/her be in control of his/her own communication environment.

Self-observation as a scientifically supported procedure

In science the idea of self-observation is a delicate matter. Natural sciences have always used observation, and more and more accurate tools have been developed for observing.

Observation of invisible phenomena is made possible by the use of tools or equipment that enable researchers to see what cannot be seen by the naked eye.

Visual representation and a highly consistent terminology are used to communicate the result of such observation processes. In linguistics observation is a means for categorizing languages and identifying different kinds of communicative behaviour; in Chomsky's framework, observation is a way for the linguist to gather and interpret incoming data according to a certain theory.

The Chomskian linguist also triggers syntactic self-observation by asking the speaker certain kinds of questions, which are intended to cause him/her to reflect and give opinions about different syntactic actualizations.

The CPP-TRS expert first promotes self-observation of himself/herself; only after this, will he/she be able to extend such process to the other individuals who will be observed. It is very clear that such a process of communicative patterns recognition has nothing to do with psychoanalytical search based on criteria external to the cognitively and linguistically based model.

Some important previous assumptions

In order to ensure that my readers, including researchers in Linguistics and in Artificial Intelligence, Cognitive Science and Information Design, understand the highly complex path I take to produce two distinct but related theories of language, it is important that I give some more information about the new theoretical and operative models I have produced.

The first step of my research is to give full recognition to a very basic fact: that language is complex. To handle such complexity, I realized immediately that existing models are a point of departure for a very long journey.

Bearing in mind the "core" and "periphery" distinction in Chomsky, it became clear to me that each of the frameworks I might refer to could take into account some processes and phenomena but that still others would be left out. Those excluded could then be described, defined and explained within a newly chosen framework, which could work as an extension of the previous one.

Each framework would then be complete in itself but still cooperate with others according to some "directionality principle" or progressive order, just like the distinction I draw between texture processes occurring before any text phenomena can take place, or text and text-segments undergoing control at a global or local level.

Just as in an engine, differing interpretative devices activate and regulate different parts, all compatible, consistent and synchronously working. Behind each of the identified devices in my Theory of Text Comprehension is a precisely reframed model of reference.

Metaphors may sound clear but they are in fact highly functionalized and precisely defined and may be turned into technical terms and conceptual tools to explain the precise processes that result in specific phenomena.

To make sure no confusion arises, what I identify as a "process" is a dynamic set of cognitive operations resulting in linguistic facts and events and communicative actions.

Phenomena are the output result of processes and therefore refer precisely to linguistic facts, events and communicative actions.

Some very important background

By closely exploring Chomsky (1957, 1965), I realized that I could share a set of very basic and important assumptions that proved to be extremely relevant to my theories. These are as follows:

1. The fundamental need to state universally valid laws in language.
2. The fundamental need to set a scientifically based framework to study language phenomena, proceeding from observation and using both description and explanation.
3. The fundamental need to represent visually dynamic aspects of language such as generation and transformations, with an adequate, consistent and consensual system.
4. The fundamental need to identify and name new and invisible transformations and movements, which work independently on each single language they apply to.
5. The fundamental need to state biologically and genetically consistent background so as to allow each individual to access a common system, both independently and compatibly with cultural and single language differences.
6. The fundamental need to state different levels such as a deep structure and a surface structure so as to justify different kinds of transformations occurring.

My approach differs from the usual in a particular sense: I neither focus on syntax, nor consider sentence as the basic unit to be working on: in my approach syntax comes last and language as such is analyzed within a more general framework that is aimed at processing linguistic sequences together with those invisible elements of natural language that are so important that if they are not taken into account properly, affect and compromise deeply any linguistic performance. As a consequence syntactic analysis will be highly beneficial because many problems will be taken care of early in the process.

On redefining 'text'

On exploring the Textlinguistics tradition, I decided that text would be the basic entity of my research work; text meaning "the basic communicative complete entity".

In the course of developing my Theory of Text Comprehension, I have introduced further specifications, by distinguishing between text and texture, text and text segments and by introducing global control text instructions and local control text execution cues.

By carefully exploring the Artificial Intelligence tradition in Knowledge Representation and in Vision, I have pushed to the extreme some basic assumptions, such as these:

Any good theory will prove to be valid if and only if it can be tested to work and be practically used. In other words, not only is it important for a theory to be based on correct and consistent assumptions to prove its validity, it needs to be operatively valid, that is, able to support consistent models, which can justify very specific aspects of linguistic performance.

I have extended the concept of visual perception to language communication: if we have pattern recognition in Vision, we can transport the same perspective into communicative pattern recognition as a way to raise the perception of such a highly complex structure as text.

Consistency in new terminology

I decided to name my new theoretical and methodological approach consistently with the target I had been addressing.

By defining my Communicative Positioning Program (CPP), I wished to convey a very precise concept:

Text and sentences represent, linguistically, a precise set of communicative functions, communicative intentions and communicative turn-taking attitudes about a certain topic.

This kind of information is conveyed not only directly by words, sentences or other linguistic elements, but comes from a so-called general interpretation process. I have named these invisible aspects of language acting together the "communicative positioning" of a certain text, which reflects the respective text producer's communicative attitude.

It took me quite a bit of time to make sure I could identify correctly and consistently the different elements, which combined create the final positioning of a certain text. First of all I had to observe, that is listen, to many commonly and naturally occurring interactions, that took place in different languages and in various cultural contexts. Next I read extensively across a variety of languages and cultures, choosing very different topics to ensure that what I had found was general enough to be declared as being universally valid. I finally had to define all of these invisible components to ensure there would be enough but not too many, that they would cover a whole variety of possible cases occurring, and that they could be combined so as to cover any kind of possible occurrence. Since these elements were not visible I also decided to make them visible so that they could be recognized and shared. I created a visual representation system for each of them, which could be both natural and intuitively understandable, once illustrated.

This is why I define as Text Representation Systems (TRS), the visual structure of different invisible elements that have become visible and represent qualitatively different phenomena.

I have created a quantum theory of language, having addressed the problem of qualitative reasoning about language first, and having recognized, analyzed, defined and carefully described qualitatively different phenomena occurring in language performance.

This is the reason why I have created different ways of representing this set of phenomena, which may actually appear all together. I have nevertheless considered that it is important to distinguish among them, even if they are actually acting together, because they have an intrinsically different nature. Not only do they differ in nature, but they also apply at different stages and at different times; this is why it is not enough to say that they all work together, because some are active inherently before others may even occur and as a precondition for the others.

A productive distinction: deep versus surface

I have re-established a productive difference between a deep structure of texture and a surface structure of text by further distinguishing between macro-level phenomena active at the deep structure level of texture (not yet linear text organization) and micro-level phenomena active at the surface structure of text (linearized text organization).

I have decided to represent the intrinsically dynamic nature of macro-level active phenomena with visual dynamic representations such as textual machines and textual canvases.

Actually, both textual canvases and textual machines are intended to represent visually and dynamically very general processes and global phenomena that are difficult to grasp in text because they occur at the texture level and only leave traces at the text level of what had previously happened at the texture level. Such global processes do nevertheless play a crucial role, because without them taking place, no surface text linear organization can even be conceived.

I can therefore state that what is left at the surface structure of text, which is already the linear organization of text in sentences and paragraphs, is the result of deep texture phenomena having occurred and having left traces.

To ensure that those traces of deep texture phenomena that I had already identified, defined and visually and dynamically represented, are correctly recognized, I proceeded carefully and progressively towards consistently naming them according to their qualitatively different nature.

I realized immediately that such traces are different in nature and therefore need to be represented in a way that will make them look what they really are: different but acting together at the surface structure of text.

By carefully exploring the nature of such traces, I can also see very clearly that they will work in a way that can be described in terms of energy.

Active energies in text processing

Within the newly established framework, I recognize some globally active energies and some locally active ones. I see no contradiction or contrast, just compatible action at different levels.

I can see that happening through a kind of respectful cooperation without interference, so that all invisible aspects of so-called textual meaning can be harmoniously carried.

The issue at this point was for me to define them and represent them visually in a way that would allow them to be seen working together, both globally and locally, as execution cues and instructions for performance.

According to these specific and different aspects, I made a preliminary distinction among communicative function, communicative intention and communicative turn-taking. These are precisely those invisible aspects of textual meaning that need to be recognized to guarantee an adequate performance.

Altogether they represent the qualitative aspect of text and text segments. In order to be able to represent global indicators for text execution, carrying communicative function, I checked many different languages and communicative contexts to make sure I had identified all the consistent and universally valid elements. I then moved towards a specific definition of each of them, attributing highly consistent terms to each of them and finally chose a set of signs that would constitute a stable and consistent syntax.

In order to represent local indicators for text execution, carrying communicative intention, I first of all checked them again very accurately to ensure that they would be enough but not too many, and that they would be consistent, thus universally valid. I then moved towards a very specific definition of each term. I finally designed a set of visual symbols which could consistently convey the previously defined concepts. I followed the very same procedure for indicating communicative turn-taking, by creating and defining another set of symbols.

As I have previously noted, communicative function, intention and turn-taking work together in text; my visual syntax based on signs and symbols allows a representation of all of these elements, which are in fact working together. In other words, signs and symbols may be combined harmoniously, without any interference or contradiction, representing qualitatively different communicative energies at work.

The 'Program'

If I had to describe with a metaphor my visual syntax for text performance, I could define my signs and symbols system both as a communicative traffic control system and as a textual notation system, where signs represent global indicators and symbols represent local execution modes. As a consistent and complete system in itself, signs and symbols may also work as a metalanguage, which may work upon any natural language and may be considered as a programming language on its own, based on a precisely defined set of instructions any native speaker should be able to recognize and apply to his/her own language.

It is important at this point for me to go back once again to the word Program that I have deliberately chosen for my CPP.

Program indicates different and highly compatible aspects in my theory.

a. The genetic cognitively consistent background for recognizing communicative positioning attitudes and for performing accordingly.
b. The set of communicative actions each individual may recognize in linguistic performance, which self-reflection gradually reveals, step by step, as if one was learning a programming language.
c. The metalanguage that operates on top of natural language, therefore constituting a programming language by itself, just as if I were using LISP or were working in a DOS environment.

This last observation allows me to indicate here the very fundamental link that exists between my theories of language and the applications I have personally designed in many fields and sent in many directions.

What I have been describing up to now largely refers to my CPP-TRS Theory of Text Comprehension. I therefore need to add that I have further developed and extended my CPP-TRS analysis so as to be able to generate a consistent CPP-TRS Theory of Text Compression, which has a direct impact in High Tech applications such as the Information Superhighways.

Designing all possible applications

I have completed and officially announced this last theory of mine, named CPP-TRS Theory of Text Compression, as well as two crucial applications, which I have named CPTRU, Communicatively Positioned-Textually Represented Unit, and CPP-TRS clip-sheet for High Speed and High Accuracy in Text Transport.

In order to compress text, even when using the CPP-TRS Theory of Text Comprehension, I have to add a new perspective to my analysis. I soon realized that I was moving from a physics-like approach to language towards a nuclear physics approach to language reactions and transformations. And a whole world of new possibilities opened in front of me! I immediately saw the tremendous implications of this new perspective.

I was already aware of the potential of my CPP-TRS Theory of Text Comprehension, especially its educational applications, high quality information processing and technical documentation and translation supports, but when I came to my CPP-TRS Theory of Text Compression, I could see that it was a real revolution not just because of its theoretical implications, but also because of its practical and tremendously powerful impact on the newest and most advanced high technologies.

A theory of language must be able to work

A specific aim of my research has been to create a theory of language that can prove its validity in practical use.

In other words, I want the linguist not just to comment on language facts or observe what is happening, but also to build communication tools and to be part of the construction of new communicative environments.

In order to do this, linguists need to share a common and accepted vocabulary, to master their own tools, just as architects do.

Architects plan first, then discuss the details of the project, then they may also take turn in what they are building, just because they can talk very specifically about what they are doing.

CPP-TRS is intended to represent a commonly shared language that can be used to refer to what is happening in natural language at a certain level.

The highly technical and precise meaning of the terminology will enable linguists to define the kind of operations they want to perform with language. Much unproductive ambiguity will then disappear, as linguists can systematically define the kind of operations they wish to perform very quickly and effectively.

CPP-TRS can thus also be viewed as a powerful metalanguage that can be used to explain and clarify what is happening within an existing scientific framework. This use of CPP-TRS is particularly useful when a framework of discussion has grown so large that it requires definite criteria both for regulating and organizing discussions and for conveying results.

This could be a tremendously powerful example for other fields, if the scientific community of linguists could reorganize certain research areas in linguistics by using criteria that could then be transferred into other research areas, as well as into the education and business fields. CPP-TRS, as a consistent way of learning what is going on behind and beyond words and sentences, may be used within any field of knowledge.

At this point the CPP-TRS encoder must commit himself or herself to the kind of interpretation he or she will actually use in his or her own text by integrating it with a consistent visual representation.

Again, using the example I have already given, and defining my proposal as a cognitive punctuation system, I reiterate that there is no contradiction between consistency and flexibility of use, consensual and natural use, stability and the need to respect the accepted interpretations that are based on individual choices about the use of the system itself.

On cognitive self-reflection

To ensure that both interpretation and encoding will result from an adequate and specific search, I have identified and named such activities as cognitive self-reflection.

Let me now spell out what I mean by this, something we were never taught but which may occasionally and randomly occur.

I want to identify and define this process because it results in something very valuable, in both its cognitive and communicative implications.

With cognitive self-reflection I will define a process of self-observation about the kinds of cognitive actions that have taken place or are taking place and result in identifiable communicative actions.

To make this process possible, those same communicative positioning attitudes that I have identified, defined and explained as CPP will support the individual during the observation process by constituting mutually shared and agreed upon interpretation cues, that can be applied to a wide and various range of cases and phenomena, according to a consistent, cognitively based and therefore universally valid syntax of language performance.

Just like language, syntax needs to be viewed as a stable system that can be a guarantee for correctness; nevertheless it allows for an infinite set of possible actualizations, in the same way that basic syntax for language performance is a guarantee for consistent interpretation of an unlimited set of texts.

Just as a syntactically correct performance may be acquired easily because of the genetic basis of a syntactic competence (Chomsky, 1957, 1965), in the very same way communicative positioning attitudes can be conceived as a consistent result of a cognitively based set of communicative attitudes that can first be recognized as active continually in one's own communicative performance in order to see and recognize them as active in the communicative performance of others.

Referring back again to Chomsky (1957, 1965), the native speaker may be able to judge and evaluate the validity, e.g. rightness, of a certain sentence according to a uniform set of rules, rules that allow a person to produce correct sentences. Those very same rules constitute a guarantee for both generation and evaluation of syntactically correct sentences.

Just as a native speaker is able to tell what is syntactically acceptable and what is not, the very same way a text performer is able to recognize the positioning he or she has attributed to his or her own text.

This recognition may be possible through so-called intuitive sensing or it may be systematically defined and scientifically based resulting from consistent, self-observation based on a set of universally valid criteria.

This is exactly what I mean by cognitive self-reflection. This may also extend to collective self-reflection, which entails precisely the interpretation of a complex set of communicative activities performed by many individuals, all together, and then being interpreted in its own variety, by using a common system of reference for interpretation.

A highly reliable system for operating text

An intrinsic advantage of a commonly shared system of reference for interpretation of communicative activities is the possibility of it constituting a solid basis for accurate requests about very specific communicative actions to be taken. In other words CPP-TRS allows any individual not only to ask about some topic but also to specify the quantity and quality of information he or she wants to be given. This is possible because the qualitative aspect of information has been recognized in CPP-TRS as playing a fundamental role in text and has therefore been declared relevant so that it can first be analyzed and then named and visually represented. Once able to identify and define the qualitative value of a given text or part of a text, any individual involved with a certain communicative intercourse will not only be able to ask for a different quantity of information, but ask also for a different quality of information about a certain topic, by defining precisely the kind of new information he/she intends to get; in other words by identifying the desired qualitative value of the requested information.

By the same principle, he/she may then also modify, add, delete or substitute parts of the text by explicitly declaring the kinds of operations he/she has been doing. Everything can be made transparent thanks to a visual, consistent system of representation that will also allow one to trace back both the kind of choices made and the procedures used. Disagreements or misunderstandings that may occur will be dealt with and solved according to the same principle: they will first be named, and described and then made transparent.

My approach may look simple but I would like to point out what "simple" means in this case.

The system —which comes as the final output of a highly complex and articulated theory— is simple because it represents the end of much complexity that has been previously recognized, dealt with and notified.

Even using the terminology and those metaphors that I have selected and redefined, it is very clear that many different approaches are involved to get to a final synthesis.

Since the aim of the Theory of Text Comprehension is to come up with a wide description, with a consistent definition and an appropriate explanation of text and text segments as communicative entities, many metaphorical frameworks have been presented in order to take care of description and definition and then proceed toward explanation. Such complexity of conceptual tools immediately raises the issue of compatibility and consistency of different models.

In order to show that I have not put together random elements, it was necessary to demonstrate how a certain framework, which has already been organized to provide description, definition and explanation for a certain set of processes and phenomena, could profitably coexist with another framework, which could take account of the description, definition and explanation of those processes and phenomena, something that could not have been taken into account in any of the previous ones.

Bridging the gap between Art and Science

Even if it may not be immediately evident, there is consistency and continuity in my research work: by referring back to Impressionism so many times in previous books (Tonfoni, 1991, 1992, 1994), I mean to relate structural changes in the art of painting to those structural changes which my theories are triggering in the art of writing. Further, I have also concentrated on light and colour, which turn out to be very important both in the CPP-TRS Theory of Text Comprehension and in the CPP-TRS Theory of Text Compression. I have visually represented communicative function, communicative intention of a text and turn-taking both statically and dynamically. I have defined communicative energy of text in terms of radiation and foreseen the possibility of reactions and structural changes in text. Futurists have been directly involved and concerned with new tools affecting their methods of painting and writing. They were so deeply fascinated by the dynamics of it that they actually intended to reproduce it in their paintings and texts. They were not scientists willing to explore the deep reasons for such phenomena; their goal was to create new special effects in painting and writing as a consequence of scientific theories and technological tools others had produced. My intention has been to do both: first I have addressed the issue of describing, defining and explaining the complexity of communicative events: in order to do that, I have created a new and highly articulated "metaphorical realm" to describe and define communicative phenomena that take place in natural language. I then proceeded to explain such phenomena by constructing a whole set of physical models and new tools, that are specifically intended to trigger new phenomena. This last part occurred after I identified and carefully analyzed those basic laws that determine current and natural communicative phenomena, just as physicists discovered that nuclear energy exists in nature and only afterwards were able to isolate it and reproduce it artificially. I have also designed a highly integrated environment for CPP-TRS text processing, which looks like a cyclotron, and which I have called Synchrocyc, as well as different tools for allowing text reactions and transformations to take place. Aware of the potential of such research, I have explicitly stated that I have not developed a new theoretical framework merely in order to solve specific problems but have designed specific applications for it. I will then direct my research into those areas which will enable my discovery and invention to contribute the most for all.

Not only is it important for a scientist to create new theories; he must also produce consistent explanations; neither is it enough to prove such theories work. The scientist must care about the application of theories and the extent to which they can be positively applied to enhance society and individual growth. This is what science should be about: the construction and sharing, or discovery and access, to the kind of knowledge that will be productive through the accurate design of a consistent technology.

This technology should be able significantly to affect the "art" of doing things, by opening up new possibilities that trigger new attitudes, aiming to amplify the potential contribution that each individual may give to humanity.

To conclude: my intention is to create a theoretical framework, that can support operational models and new tools, which I have intended to design, that will enhance responsibility and awareness in the communication and information processing era.

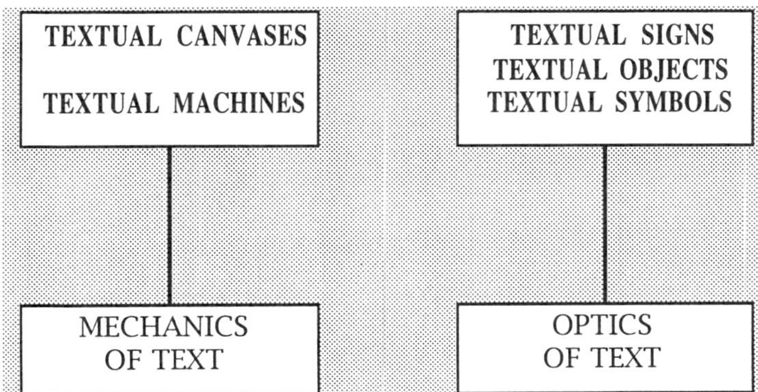

Figure 1. CPP-TRS Theory of Text Comprehension (Tonfoni, 1989-94)

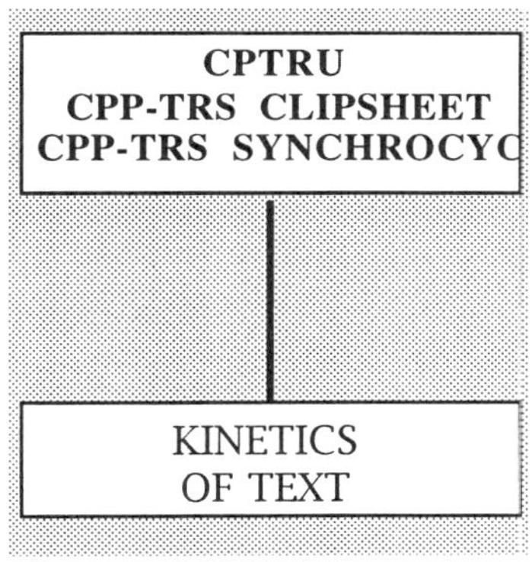

Figure 2. CPP-TRS Theory of Text Compression (Tonfoni, 1995)

I have visually summarized the CPP-TRS system's components in the following Figures 1 and 2 respectively. A more extensive explanation of terms can be found in the second, third and fourth sections of this book and in the bibliography.

Part Two
Introduction to Physics of Language

Communicative attitude, cognitive aptitude and textual actitude

Let me explain why I decided to establish a clear-cut distinction between "attitude" and "aptitude".

By the basic assumption I made about the natural and consistent ability of the individual to trace back his or her communicative positioning attitudes and to recognize other individuals' communicative positioning attitudes, I can define cognitive aptitude as the corresponding cognitive ability that allows individuals consistently to recognize what is going on in language as a reflection of what is possible owing to a commonly shared program.

Cognitive structures are based on cognitive aptitudes; they allow communicative attitudes to occur and to reflect on natural language as communicative patterns, which may be recognized as such, because they are cognitively grounded and commonly shared. They manifest themselves in texture on a dynamic level and in text as a final state resulting from texture processes, which can be traced back. In the CPP-TRS framework the newly and precisely defined terminology I have introduced, as well as the visual representation apparatus, are specifically aimed at creating a possibility for exploiting and exploding the visibility of all such phenomena, which can only be seen at the text level and may be observed through a process of self-reflection.

The transparency of such important processes and phenomena are significant conditions for a consistent explanation at different levels. The visual apparatus, together with the text it relates to, is a powerful device for an understanding of all of the communicative energies that are active in text that can consistently produce understanding.

This is how I came to use the peculiar term "actitude", which applies to text to indicate communicative energies that actively produce consistent understanding.

Textual actitude is the communication and information energy potential and can be processed in very different ways. It may be left visible at the surface level, as it appears in a textual pentagram, where text is being complemented by the visual execution cues, thereby allowing for consistent execution and for execution changes. These may be made explicit by using the visual apparatus dynamically, like passing from one style to another, by declaring the nature of the changes with the corresponding CPP-TRS visual representation, either on a local or global level. Going back to the metaphor I have chosen, this looks like a kind of text X-raying process. But there is another, extremely powerful way to use communication energy, similar to what happens in nuclear energy. This is the possibility of manipulating previously CPP-TRS processed textual units in order first to compress them both quantitatively and qualitatively and then proceed to any kind of reaction like acceleration and aggregation, which looks like fusion or fission.

Cognitive aptitudes and communicative attitudes belong to the Theory of Text Comprehension, whereas textual actitudes refer to the Theory of Text Compression.

Full exposure and obscuration in text processing

I have already thoroughly illustrated how a textual pentagram may be thought of as full exposure to textual communicative energy in the sense that it makes visible what was previously invisible. In my Theory of Text Comprehension there are other ways to explode the visibility of those qualitative aspects of communication, which are normally left invisible in text.

This is why I kept consistency, continuity and contiguity among the different parts of my visual apparatus. To give an example, let me mention the possibility of a "soft use" of signs as indication cues for global text execution versus a "hard use" of these as indicators for qualitatively different communicative space in textual origami.

There is a gradation in enlightenment of information, which does not compromise the consistency of qualitative meaning attribution.

Another example: textual signs may harmoniously lead toward 3-D representation of textual global functions as in the case of textual objects.

Full exposure to qualitative aspects of communication may lead to full expansion of text communicative energy potential, resulting in textual forms, by having previously undergone a process of text virtualization and conversion. I have thoroughly explained such concepts within an operational research framework.

Let me now explain what I mean by the term "obscuration".

By obscuration I mean the intentional process of turning a textual pentagram or a textual information territory into a pentagram or a territory which is either partially or totally lacking in light or illumination. This is a deliberate evasion of clarity in two different ways:

1. A textual pentagram is obscurated if
   a. *some parts of it are lacking qualitative information cues for consistent execution*
   b. *some changes in text execution cues do not show traces of the originally proposed execution cues. Thus the textual pentagram can be said to be lacking illumination.*
2. A textual information territory is obscurated if
   a. *CPTRU, which means the quantitatively and qualitatively compressed textual unit, only shows qualitative communication cues as indexing and retrieving cues*
   b. *CPTRU, having undergone a process of acceleration and reaction, does not show traces of the processes having occurred. In this way the textual information territory can be declared to be lacking in light. All of the described phenomena are intrinsically extremely dangerous because they cause partial or even total loss of the information sources, removing control from the entire operation.*

What my system does is to keep all the information energies transformation and execution cues ready and available all the time. However I must provide information about the possible risks, which may occur if obscuration takes place, so that such emergency situations will never occur, or may be properly handled through understanding, awareness and social commitment on the part of the scientist.

New evidence, new theories and new terminology

In physics it is extremely important to take into account the theory behind a certain experiment and model. Many important observations made by physicians in the past are lost because we do not have information about their framework of interpretation. In physics, any good experiment is based on the tools the observer has used and on conceptual structure upon which the observer has reframed experiences and experiments. It is also very important to distinguish between "prejudiced observation of facts" and "high perception of phenomena"; the first attitude being extremely damaging for any kind of scientific work, the second being a correct attitude toward analyzing a certain experience so as to achieve a detailed knowledge of a certain fact or phenomenon.

The perception of a certain fact or phenomenon should lead to the reproduction of the same or of an equivalent. A "high perception" will only be possible if it is grounded upon a clear-cut, coherent and concise symbolic representation system. What I have defined as "textual perception" is exactly the kind of attitude a language scientist should be able to adopt in order to observe, experience and process text, text being considered the basic entity to which observation and analysis will apply.

"Textual perception" in CPP-TRS is based on the complete system of visualization and definition, which is subject to some "directionality principle" in the sense that some components have been observed and represented as working before others.

There is a clear distinction between identifying common sense laws of meaning and physical laws of syntactic structure and communicative energies. Some observation of facts by the use of natural tools is enough to establish "true or false" conditions about statements for common sense knowledge representation based on agreed and consensually shared experience. Physical laws of language are not based merely on experience but on experiments as well, which means that different conceptual frameworks and observation criteria will be adopted at different times; their nature is therefore intrinsically different and the "true or false" condition cannot always be considered as a valid classification criterion to decide about the rightness or adequacy of a certain model. What really matters is the kind of control on the quality of both experience and observation and the degree of approximation, which may vary considerably according to the power of observational tools which are being used. Research on common sense and knowledge representation in language is based on a stable "platform" that rests on the fact that abstract terms, properties and attributes are linked to real objects, facts and experiences.

This is why we see a relatively fast development of highly productive knowledge representation models and theories in the field of Artificial Intelligence, based on strong and powerful concepts such as frame (Minsky, 1975), script (Schank, 1977), plan (Wilensky, 1983) and plot unit (Lehnert, 1981).

A common sense law is a general assertion which may be either true or false and which can be tested and confronted with reality directly; as a result of such testing, it may be declared to be either correct or incorrect, and if it is accepted, it will be added to a whole other set of assertions. Research aimed at exploring energies and forces active in language, both at a syntactical level and at a communicative level, is based on symbolic representation, which may be more or less adequate and continuously evolving, owing to the evolution of the theories it is based upon. Any symbolic representation is strictly connected to a certain theory; this is why it is so important to relate each term and element explicitly to the specific theory that is being adopted. Otherwise much confusion and ambiguity may be generated as a result of meanings attributed to a certain term that is used differently according to a different perspective.

Old evidence, new evidence

It is very important for a scientist, and particularly for a language scientist, to be aware of the terminological consequences derived from newly acquired evidence about certain facts and of the possible ambiguity that ordinary terminology may generate if the basic assumptions have changed.

If I were to define the CPP-TRS framework as belonging to pragmatics tout court, the only aspect that would result in a correct interpretation would be the literal meaning of "pragma", meaning "activity" and "action"; my theory being based on the assumption that text is the basic communicative active entity. Pragmatics today is mostly related to descriptive analysis, hence it would be difficult to define my approach in such terms.

Further, there is an animated and interesting discussion in the field about what a "text" really is as opposed to "discourse", resulting in a wide variety of opinions.

My view radically differs from others because of the introduction of a "quantum mentality" in language analysis, text being the complete, therefore active, communication entity. A Quantum Theory of Language applies better to some substantial changes of perspective that are specifically related to linking together the qualitative and the quantitative aspects of text.

I find the Chomskian dichotomy between "deep structure" and "surface structure" still to be a valid one because it covers those substantial differences between the "potential" and the "actual". As a consequence of such productive distinction I have introduced the dichotomy between "texture" and "text".

The verb "cognize" was introduced by Chomsky to mean "knowing the grammar of a language", the verb "know" being too general and therefore ambiguous.

I have introduced "recognize" to mean "know the positioning of a certain text based on a commonly shared cognitive program", the verb referring both to self-recognition and cognitive awareness. Terminology can therefore be reframed or extended or radically substituted when the term has such a long tradition. Adding one more definition would certainly slow down the process of correct interpretation and use, resulting in an ineffective way of identifying and expressing newly acquired evidence.

Nevertheless, some connection with the traditional framework may be productive: classical physics and quantum physics have shown so many commonalities that some apparently contradictory concepts have been found to be compatible at the end such as in the case of corpuscular and wavelike theories of matter. Thus, I am not proposing the CPP-TRS framework as contradicting the classical statements of Linguistics or Knowledge Representation Research, but as a compatible framework for a more global interpretation of communicative events. My explicit intention has always been to explain complex invisible aspects of language and knowledge representation through simple, visible and consistent interpretation cues.

Abstract theories and mechanical models

If we analyze thoroughly what has been going on in Physics for centuries, we can see an alternation of abstract theories and mechanical models, developed to explain observable or unobservable facts and events.

If the main issue in the science of language is not categorizing facts but creating a consistent representation of what is behind language facts and events, there should be no contradiction at all in alternating and harmoniously combining abstract theories and mechanical models of specific facts and processes.

No doubt there cannot merely be an exclusive and global theory of language but only different theories acting at different levels that can be applied to different kinds of problems.

Generalizing and identifying common rules is a typical result of abstract theories aimed at a need for economy, whereas mechanical models are aimed at capturing a certain fact by reproducing it or analogyzing at different levels.

Representation turns out to be a highly productive aspect both for abstraction and for modelling: within a CPP-TRS framework, visual representation is specifically intended to be explanatory in order to be turned into a set of operational devices for solving qualitatively different problems. Since facts and processes, which are analyzed, can be both simple and complex, those visual representation systems that I have designed do reflect such structural difference and are therefore qualitatively different. For this very reason they differ at a basic level: canvases and machines are aimed at representing complex, dynamic and therefore "scruffy" processes in primary text organization.

Signs and symbols are designed to represent the final result of such processes in a stable, detailed and "neat" way.

The diversity of such representation systems is actually the guarantee that the inherently different communication phenomena and processes being analyzed have been completely distinguished one from the other.

One more aspect needs to be pointed out: simple facts may result in more complex combinations and may need to be observed in order to be defined and explained when active as a combination. Facts that look static may merely be the end result of a dynamic set of processes that occurred earlier or are still occurring.

Such dishomogeneity is not to be considered an inconsistency; it is rather a proof that correct definitions of dishomogeneous facts and processes are occurring.

The term dishomogeneous should be replaced by terms such as "complex" so as not to suggest any negative connotation. If simple facts or processes may be isolated and identified as such, then a consistent representation may be found; if they tend to operate as a combination, a consistent representation should take into account the whole system of facts and processes in a dynamic way and a consistent and qualitatively different kind of representation should be found. Mechanical models are particularly suited in this case, because they can animate highly complex processes involving different energies and forces active simultaneously, by keeping the right progression. This is why I have designed my textual machines. If there is some overlap in my mechanical models, this should not cause concern; some energies are active in more than one of the described facts and phenomena, and therefore need to be represented and modelled at different times to be recognized. This may be considered as a "realistic" representation in the sense that it will support complex language phenomena; given the assumption that forces and energies of different kinds are always active in language at different levels. The "language matter" may therefore change, altering properties at a structural level, with real changes occurring when exposed to such forces and energies — like iron undergoing magnetism. Forces and energies are the qualitative aspect of communication, and deeply and intrinsically affect the language structure. In my CPP-TRS framework I have always felt the need to talk about text in terms of differing energy states and this has proved to be very productive in order to distinguish among the qualitatively different natures of the phenomena and processes being observed.

Creating qualitatively different models to justify and explain qualitatively different communicative facts and communicative actions guarantees that qualitatively different problems will not be mixed.

Language, Information and Communication

All the way through my research work I have looked to etymology, as with it, it is often possible to find evidence to support very strong scientific claims.

Information — from latin "informo" — means literally to give shape, shape up. Information is the process through which knowledge, coming from different experiences, is organized in different forms and formats. As a consequence of such processes, information may be referred to as a certain kind of "matter". Natural language is one of the three major states or phases of that matter, which is information, the others being visual languages and gestural languages. Each state of information has properties that distinguish it from the others and is therefore independent of the particular "substance" being studied.

By "substance" I mean the specific linguistic unit being analyzed in the specific language.

Semiotics is largely concerned with the study and description of the different properties that characterize each of the major states or phases, which are currently named as "codes" (Eco, 1975; Sebeok, 1960).

Semiotics, at least up to the present time, has never been concerned with processes such as transformation of properties in order to generate new complex units, as it is largely concerned with the interpretation of observable phenomena and the consistent description of facts. This approach is of great significance and I am certainly not diminishing it in its valuable contribution. Rather, I am defining the range of problems that are being addressed and handled in such a way. All kinds of information is in the form of information units of different sizes and qualities.

A visual information unit will differ from a gestural information unit or a natural language information unit, just like a gaseous state differs from a liquid state and a solid state, yet all of them are "states of matter".

All kinds of information consist of simple and complex units that can be interpreted through a highly articulated process, involving a certain set of cognitive processes. The different states of information have properties which make them look different at some times, so that not even the same terminology can be used unless it is carefully defined and specified, because not even a common set of problems is being addressed. It would not really make much sense to address the problem of summarizing a gestural sequence or a few icons with the same terms we would use for summarizing a novel or a narrative text using natural language; this would not give us an economical system of interpretation since we would be referring to qualitatively different processes. Drawing distinctions among different states of the same matter by applying radically different but still compatible systems for both representation and interpretation is a widely accepted, highly productive practice in physics; it actually produces no confusion and provides much clarity. Even the same phenomenon may be described and defined by two apparently different frameworks that are compatible and, at the end, productive, as in the case of corpuscular and wavelike theories of matter.

This gave me good reason to think of the different kinds of representation systems that can be applied to a very complex linguistic entity such as "text".

I like to postulate qualitatively different kinds of interpretation and understanding as well, because the existence of such processes is supported by evidence.

Interpreting and understanding a natural language sequence is substantially different from interpreting and understanding a visual language or a gestural language sequence.

To differentiate among such aspects of interpretation and understanding, I have postulated the existence of linear-sequential interpretation and understanding processes and global-vibrational interpretation and understanding processes. Such differences will become clear in the course of my exposition.

There are cases where information particles that have been identified in each of the previously mentioned information states may be considered to be relatively independent of the influence of nearby particles, whereas in other cases they may be found to be subordinated to forces exerted on them by neighbours.

Forces and energies are communication elements because they apply to information segments and units of different kinds in order to produce qualitatively different communication effects.

It is difficult to establish a clear distinction between information and communication, just as it is hard to draw a line between the particle-like and the wave-like nature of natural language.

These are interconnected: as such they manifest themselves in different but consistent ways in the three major states or phases that were first introduced, that is in natural language, visual language and gestural language.

Both concepts of information and communication (latin informo, shape up and communis facio, put something in common) imply a dynamic process taking place in various steps and through different kinds of operations. In some ways I would like to state that communication forces and energies act upon information units in such a way as to turn them into informactive units, where the information potential is actualized.

I will further explore the concept of informactivity when I present the possibility of both recognizing and producing transformations and reactions in textually represented information territories.

Communicative forces and energies active upon language

When certain kinds of communicative forces and energies become active in natural language, not only do they affect and determine the positioning of a certain text by influencing each text unit pervasively but they also have an impact on the syntactic structure. This last assertion will certainly help linguists working within the Chomskian framework recognize some aspects of movement such as binding, move α and so on.

This certainly needs further direct exploration in order that it be practically used to solve some of the as yet unsolved problems.

Text segments and text units of natural language in a certain communicative space or context may be considered to collide with one another and rebound to produce different kinds of interpretation and understanding.

A very important property of the natural language state of information is that it is able to represent any kind of content whatever communicative space it is put in, where communicative space means the context. Other important properties of the natural language state of information are the following: 1) text segments, text units and texts may be compressed at a local or global level when synthesis is being applied; 2) text segments, text units and texts may be expanded at a local or global level when analysis is being applied; 3) text segments, text units and texts may be condensed at a local or global level, to a concept or a set of concepts, when abstraction applies.

If these changes take place, they affect the nature of the original text segment, text unit or text in a way that will reflect on the interpretation and understanding of the text segment, text unit or text.

I have called "pressure" the way the communicative positioning of a text segment, text unit or text reflects on the information structure of a text segment, text unit or text, which I have called "temperature".

Pressure is therefore applied to the specific communicative component of text, whereas temperature is applied to the specific informative component.

I can make a further statement, which I have conceived as a kind of physical law of text temperature and pressure balancing, where any change of temperature leads to pressure changes, and vice versa.

This is how the quantitative aspect of text, which is the information structure, and the qualitative aspect, which is the communication energy, can be harmoniously linked together but which can be conceived as both an informative and a communicative entity.

Changes in temperature and pressure occur all the time and they can now not only be noticed but observed, measured and analyzed very accurately within the new CPP-TRS framework.

A macroscopic view and a microscopic view of language

In order to be able to observe and explain qualitatively different phenomena and facts about language, both a macroscopic view and a microscopic view are needed.

A macroscopic view is specifically represented by my CPP-TRS framework, which is connected but independent of an atomic theory of language like a syntactic one.

By "connected" I mean the very important relationships that exist between the analysis of the positioning and representation and its reflections upon the syntactic structures; by "independent" I mean that it can be analyzed and explained by referring to internal and specific parameters.

A macroscopic view deals with specific properties, which can be both identified and measured and which are based on particles determining the pressure of a text.

Such description of textuality in terms of measurable properties I define as "phenomenological thermodynamics of text" and "text transport theory".

The phenomenological thermodynamics of text is largely concerned with information distribution and information structure of a text segment, text unit or text, in other words with the text temperature.

The text transport theory is largely concerned with the reflection of the communicative positioning of a text segment, text unit or text, in other words with the text pressure.

Both phenomenological thermodynamics of text and text transport theory have precise representation systems in my CPP-TRS framework. More specifically, I have represented phenomenological thermodynamics with my canvases and tapestry and fresco text representation systems, while I have represented text transport theory with my textual machines.

Textual canvases and tapestry and fresco on the one hand and textual machines on the other share the same property of representing macrophenomena, which are complex and "scruffy", and which represent processes evolving in different stages.

They represent some basic actions that work before the text is shaped; the actualized text keeps traces of such fundamental processes or movements that occur through a different kind of text representation system, one which is more stabilized and which corresponds to my textual pentagram system, based on signs and symbols.

Both kinds of processes in any case have an impact on the syntactic structure in a very positive sense: some phenomena that are hard to handle syntactically because they refer to something external (which Chomsky has recognized many times as part of "discourse" or referred to as pragmatics), can be easily handled within a text phenomenological thermodynamics or a text transport theory so that when it comes to their syntactic manifestation they have already been explained. Some difficulties arising within a syntactic framework are due to the fact that some problems are addressed that would be more easily solved after having been addressed in the terms I have suggested.

A microscopic view deals with the description of sentence phenomena, of specific language facts on a syntactic level and with the explanation of rules regulating such phenomena.

An explanation of a system of interacting rules is also required in order to justify the observed behaviour of a language speaker when studied in a laboratory. The most powerful model of this now existing is Chomsky's framework.

I would like to define his theory in terms of kinetic theory of syntax, because Chomsky has identified movement existing in the syntactic structure.

I want to repeat that both a macroscopic view and a microscopic view are needed to explain highly complex phenomena, which manifest themselves in natural language. I can also foresee advantages deriving from the strong link existing between the two views, resulting in raising the power of both views to explain qualitatively different phenomena of the same nature, which is natural language.

I would also like to push my assertions about Chomsky's theory a bit further: not only did he create a kinetic theory of syntax but he also configured a statistical thermodynamics of syntax. I will now clarify in which sense this last assertion of mine should be interpreted.

Cognitive structures, knowledge structures, syntactic structures

The reason why I have postulated the existence of cognitive structures is that cognitive processes like focalization, selection and so on, create specific effects on natural language that are clearly different from those we can find active in visual or gestural languages. By this, if I say something such as "focus on that part of the image", I really mean some cognitive operation, which is substantially the same but has different implementation modes according to the state or phase of information to which it applies.

Cognitive structures can therefore be defined as dynamic structures built on cognitive processes manifesting themselves via natural language. Going back to the previous example, focusing is different in nature when it manifests itself in natural language or in vision: iconic focusing differs from textual topic focusing.

In order to differentiate and still retain the same terminology to define each of those cognitive processes, I found it necessary to refer back to the existence of cognitive structures that are the output results of cognitive processes having been applied to the natural language state of information. I also like to abbreviate the term "cognitive structures" — which is by definition plural because of the many different cognitive processes that are involved — into the term "co-structures".

"Co-structures" are intrinsically dynamic; it is important to keep the dynamic aspect of representation active all the time in order to explain and justify complex phenomena, which are part of a more general linguistic theory. Co-structures become the dynamic grounding upon which language facts can be consistently built. They neither interfere nor diminish the role syntactic structures play; they merely reinforce and support them.

I would also like to add that they make possible the actual functioning of knowledge structures such as the Frame (Minsky, 1975), the Script (Schank, 1977), the Plan (Wilensky, 1983), and the Plot Unit (Lehnert, 1981). Knowledge Representation Structures such as the above need in any case to be activated at some point on the basis of a structured organization, which can be dynamic.

Co-structures may allow both the syntactic representation component and the knowledge representation component to be harmoniously and synchronously active.

Only through the harmonious merging of the different components can we expect to handle such complex problems as language facts. I have always tried to give physical examples of undefined and invisible problems such as those raised by language. This is why I have created my CPP-TRS framework and produced qualitatively distinct visual representation systems such as canvas, machines and so on. Taking into account the need to create a physical example that may work like a model of the above mechanism based on different structures and which allows a full interpretation and understanding of natural language texts to take place, let me offer the charging machinery for handling natural language.

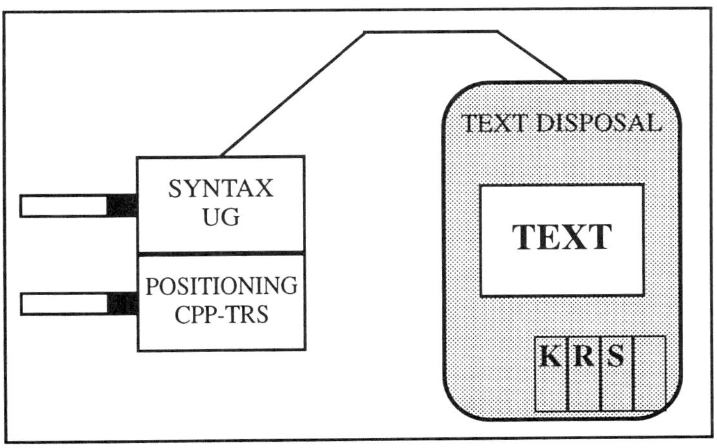

Figure 1.

Let us now have a look at Figure 1. What I want to represent visually with the charging machinery for handling information in a natural language state is the built-in syntactic component, represented by the Universal Grammar (UG), and the positioning program (CPP-TRS), which are plugged directly into the mind; they are both linked to an external disposal which is made of the knowledge representation systems (KRS) that are acquired through experience and therefore not found in the mind originally.

When a text comes in, it will be charged on the text disposal. This will become active as UG and CPP-TRS fill with the energy that allows the KRS component to become active. The KRS component may be partially active even if UG and CPP-TRS are not plugged in but in order to get the full charging to reach interpretation and understanding of the text at some point, UG and CPP-TRS will have to be plugged in.

This is all due to the diversified activation of syntactic structures, co-structures and knowledge structures, based on different parameters.

In language understanding we can also differentiate among different kinds of expectations, which are respectively syntactic expectations, positioning expectations and knowledge representation expectations.

Syntactic expectations can be handled within a kind of Case Grammar (Fillmore 1977), which needs still some further extension in order to cope with a wide variety of syntactical facts. Syntactic expectations can also be handled accurately and productively within a Chomskian framework.

Positioning expectations need to be accurately described. Some kind of positioning expectation may have to be found in the relationship, which exists between and among textual functional indicators on a global level.

In other words, a textual sign may create the expectation for another one to come either before or afterward. An example of expectation driven syntax for textual functional indicators is represented by the sequence inscribed arcs-opened text space.

For such sequences I think in terms of an "If-Then rule". Other sequences are weaker and certainly not deterministic.

Links between and among text styles indicators are almost non-existent and extremely weak.

Links between text styles indicators and text turn-taking indicators are again extremely weak and almost non-existent.

Links between textual functional indicators and both text-styles and text turn-taking indicators offer some rather weak predictions, but only tentative ones and certainly not deterministic.

Knowledge representation expectations have been widely explored within the Artificial Intelligence tradition of knowledge representation and in common sense; we certainly know that the strongest expectations are context driven and I would point the reader to bibliography on these very issues rather than discuss them here. Another point of relevance in order better to specify the nature of co-structures versus knowledge structures is the level of familiarity and the way it affects positioning detection.

Communicative Patterns Recognition

Before discussing the specific issue of communicative patterns recognition based upon co-structures, let me first go back to the question of familiarity versus unfamiliarity.

Familiarity with knowledge structures may certainly help identify the positioning through an appropriate communicative patterns recognition process. Context assessment and recognition is crucial as well. Let me now give an example, which comes from a personal experience.

I was at a conference in Italy, speaking to an Italian colleague who was also giving a talk. During a coffee break,I wanted to tell him that I had submitted a proposal for a scientific paper that I had first published in English, to be published in Italian. Here is our conversation:

I: I have just submitted a proposal for the translation of my paper, which has already been translated.

He: Oh good. It is our old back-and-forth between the two languages.

To understand this short conversation, some contextual information is needed.

By identifying the consistent positioning, you may grasp something more, which refers to the situation the two of us share: scientists having to cope with the fact that Italian scientists have to work in two languages to be understood in Italy and to obtain an international audience.

If we were to define the positioning out of the text sequence, the attribution would be that of "analogous story".

My colleague was referring to an analogous experience he had gone through himself, writing English papers and translating them into Italian. He was analogizing and referring to a commonly shared experience.

Conversational implications are a help but there is something more needed to achieve a deep understanding. In other words, they would not be enough, because pragmatics is merely acting in a classification mode and very much at a level of description as it deals with different contexts.

According to a CPP-TRS perspective, the so-called positioning represents a kind of universal grammar for different communicative actions, reflecting on different languages, in different ways and which can still be recognized by native speakers through communicative patterns recognition.

An explanatory theory of Pragmatics

Much research going on today in pragmatics is on context driven communicative patterns observation and description.

It is important and valuable work which corresponds to the linguistic categorization search, which was previously done at a descriptive level before the Chomskian revolution.

Much observational data are important on a descriptive level, and up to now pragmatics has been largely concerned with descriptive matters.

In order to create an explanatory theory, however, what is needed is a highly complex and articulated system having well defined parameters and points of reference. This is what has happened in the realm of syntactic analysis with Chomsky's framework.

As a consequence of a real complexity, we can see how the same framework has evolved in time, without denying the basic scientific assumptions upon which it was based. The need to define a really consistent Universal Grammar has never been disproved by problems or difficulties.

The CPP-TRS approach intends to be an explanatory theory of pragmatics in two different ways.

First, the CPP-TRS Theory of Text Comprehension is an explanatory theory of language as an information phase which is communicatively active and which justifies the naturally occurring communicative facts represented by texts and texts segments.

The CPP-TRS Theory of Text Comprehension deals with actual texts and actual performance.

Second, the CPP-TRS Theory of Text Compression, which is a consistent output of the CPP-TRS Theory of Text Comprehension, has become so powerful that it can generate and transform naturally produced texts and text segments into ideal CPTRU — and CPTRU territories.

In some ways CPP-TRS is a generative and transformational theory of language activities, but only in a very special sense.

CPP-TRS can interpret naturally generated texts and text segments based on a set of interpretative devices that act upon different levels and represent qualitatively different processes and phenomena occurring in natural language.

Those interpretative devices that I have defined and visually represented are so consistent that they can be transparently used in combination with natural language as a visual system for reinforcing natural language itself.

As interpretation devices they can be used dynamically to indicate transformations occurring in natural language, largely as reformulation both globally and locally.

As such they show existing processes by labelling the qualitative information about the nature of such processes.

As a consequence of a high consistency of representation, the CPP-TRS model is so powerful that it can generate its own text segments as texts based on those communicative energies that are found in natural language intercourses.

This is where CPP-TRS is a tremendously powerful mechanism for autonomous processes of generation and transformation.

CPTRU is the kernel textual unit keeping communicative energy and information force active and ready to be modified through reactions that may occur more or less locally.

Comparison with nuclear processes here becomes extremely powerful.

Deep knowledge of the material and mastering of different techniques

I have always been intrigued by the basic principles that determine the intimate structure of different substances and which change my intuitions into deep knowledge of causes enabling me to generate theories supported by operatively valid models.

In order to do this, the "material" needs to be split and cut in order to penetrate it.

Lucretius in De Rerum Natura provides a good example of visionary intuitions based on the construction of a metaphor which is then turned into scientific descriptions and explanations of physical phenomena.

The physical realm I have studied is language and I have begun by observing language artifacts, such as texts.

Some may wonder why a physical theory of language comes to be linked to a set of interpretative techniques that I have presented through the metaphors of painting, architecture and music.

I now want to explain this link by referring to what happens in painting when the painter starts to think about the chemical properties of his paints. It is one thing to paint with oil, another to paint with gouache.

Each has properties that deeply affect the product that will result from using them.

Differing molecular structures in painting affect light reflections as well as changes that occur in the chemical nature over time. From this point I begin to analyze the different properties of the various information states, specifically concentrating on natural language both at a macro-level and at a micro-level of observation.

As for architecture, let us focus on the need architects have to know about the intrinsic properties of the material that are to be used, both physically and chemically. Nothing can be planned or even conceived if the nature of the material has not been taken into account and thoroughly explored.

As for music, nothing is arbitrary: everything can be described, defined, conveyed and executed according to a very specific plan based on a highly technical notation system. Switching harmoniously from one paradigm and frame of reference into another one allows a scientific approach to be both rigorous and unconstrained by just one particular view.

The greatest Italian artists in the fifteenth century were all very much in touch with the material they used and familiar with a wide set of substances, arts, techniques and different ways of doing things. Further, they were scientists as well because they knew the theories behind and beyond what they were doing. We should never forget Leonardo Da Vinci's motto "Studia prima la scienza e poi seguita la pratica nata da essa Scienza".

Communicative energy and text perception

Just as light can be considered to be "responsible" for sight, communication energy can be considered "responsible" for text perception, which means understanding of text. Text is the actualization of that specific state of information that is natural language.

It is interesting to analyze the interaction between communicative energy and information in each of the three different states in which information may appear: natural language, visual language and gestural language.

I will concentrate on the interaction between communicative energy and natural language, which is actualized in textures, texts, text segments and text units respectively.

It will, of course, be very interesting to explore other kinds of interaction as well as to note the difference between the "communicative charging" a linguistic text may show and a visual text or gestural sequence.

CPP-TRS in any case is able to work on top of such texts.

Just as physicists talk about light propagation in terms of both particles and waves, scientists of language may consider wave-like phenomena of communicative energy propagation in text to be completely compatible with particle-like syntactic phenomena within the newly established Quantum Theory of Language.

Communicative energy is a form of energy conveyed through the textual space at a certain velocity, without necessarily transporting the matter, which is the actual text or parts of it; traces are in any case left to help one to recognize the nature of the communicative energy at any given time.

Just as with light, a text or a text segment may absorb, reflect and refract communicative energy in a certain way before it reaches the text observer.

The human textual perception system is able to extract a part of the information, which comes with the text or text segment.

Through the use of textual instruments such as those I have created within my CPP-TRS framework — textual machines, textual canvases, textual signs, textual symbols and textual objects — the text observer will be able to raise his/her own textual perception significantly.

I like to define my CPP-TRS tools as spectroscopic instruments for communicative energy and information detection, just as telescopes and microscopes extract extremely important information from the environment which the human eye alone could not possibly obtain.

When communicative energy is incident, in a perpendicular direction, on a text or text segment (i.e. that it shows itself explicitly with the corresponding definition), it will be transmitted directly. For example, this is what happens when showing a comment on a certain fact.

This is a comment on the actual political situation in Italy.

(CPP-TRS: 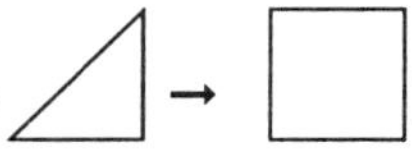).

But this is rarely the case. Most of the time communicative energy reflects on a text or a text segment and it is far easier to recognize communicative energy after a certain interpretative process has occurred, as in the following example:

I'd like to give you my opinion about a certain set of events occurring in Italy today. I am talking about the political situation and I want to tell you what I think.

(CPP-TRS: 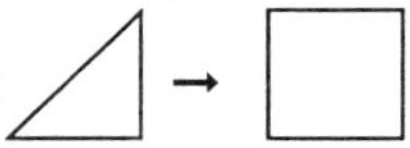).

With a particle-like theory of syntax, there would be serious problems in justifying communicative energy taking different forms in text.

If communicative energy consists of a stream of particles (lexical items or sentences) all alike, because like cause should produce like effects, it cannot be explained why some particles are communicatively charged and others are not. With a wave-like theory of text it is easy to explain that the velocity of communicative energy transmission may vary because it is the result of wavelength frequency, which may vary as well.

This last point helps us understand the relevance of a particle–wave-like theory of text in my CPP-TRS theory of Text Compression which is based on qualitative reasoning about communication and information.

Mechanical effects of communicative energy

Up to now I have pointed out the relevance of qualitative phenomena and qualitative reasoning about text, which represents the entity to be analyzed in the information state natural language.

However, relevant quantitative changes and phenomena will also take place in communicative energy transmission and should be taken into account because they are extremely relevant.

I define such phenomena as mechanical effects of communicative energy.

When communicative energy is either emitted or absorbed by a text or text segment, three mechanical effects take place:

1. an exchange of information density in sentences or paragraphs
2. an exchange of sentences and paragraphs linear distribution
3. an exchange in the syntactic structure of sentences.

Those quantitative changes that may result in reductions, expansions or reformulations of the actual text may manifest themselves in the following ways:

1. topic-comment shifts
2. subordination and coordination shifts
3. ellipsis or elliptical phenomena.

These are quite radical quantitative phenomena, which are generated as a consequence of the qualitative phenomena, that were explored earlier.

All of these effects can be explained partially within a classical particle theory of syntax and globally within a quantum theory of text. As a matter of fact, it is by referring to the particle–wave-like theory of text that those phenomena can be explored in relation to exchanges between communicative energy and both texts and text segments at a macro-level or as interactions between and among sentences at a micro-level.

My CPP-TRS electromagnetic theory of language communication approaches communicative energy by explicitly recognizing and stating that every detector of communicative energy (textual machines, textual canvases, textual objects, textual signs and textual symbols) is also a communicative transducer and converter.

By the Quantum Theory of Language we can state that absorption of communicative energy is a continual process.

Communicative energy can be exchanged in infinitesimal amounts between sentences and both coordinate and subordinate clauses by keeping an information equilibrium, where equilibrium is a dynamic concept.

A sentence may exist only in one of a set of discrete stationary states of information.

Information has some internal energy of its own before it is charged by communicative energy as well; information energy is substantially different from communicative energy, so to distinguish it, I will call it informative force.

Just as in physics, informative forces are able to determine acceleration, as we will see in those text-acceleration processes that I have been able to determine through my CPP-TRS.

Chomsky (1980) stated that "linguistic knowledge, of course, extends beyond the level of the sentence. We know how to construct discourses of various sorts, and there are no doubt principles governing discourse structure".

Even though he focuses on sentence and syntax, Chomsky has recognized the need to explain principles governing a qualitatively and not merely a quantitatively different linguistic entity such as discourse. The need further to explore the qualitatively different nature of the components led me to the formulation of an Active Theory of Information as well as of a Theory of Communicative Energy. It is possible in physics and in natural philosophy, as Faraday defines it, that various observable forces are intimately interconnected, for example electric current produces magnetic force and vice versa. Similarly in the physics of language, communicative energies affect information forces and vice versa.

As I have previously illustrated, natural language is one of the three major states or phases of information, the others being visual and gestural languages. Each state of information has properties that distinguish it from the others, and are therefore independent of the particular sentence or text being analyzed. All languages consist of sentences, more or less complex, involving a lower or higher set of embedded clauses and texts. Understanding occurs through a textual space and is dynamic in nature.

On a purely syntactic level of analysis, each sentence can be analyzed and parsed virtually independently of the influence of nearby sentences; but at a textual level each sentence is subordinated to the information forces exerted by the wider textual space as well as to the communicative energies active upon the text.

From Theory of Binding to Theory of Bonding without contradictions

Sentence parsing at a purely syntactic level is bound by very precise rules. If we move to discourse processing involving sequences of sentences, we still see collision phenomena occurring and dynamics between and among sentences.

All syntactic phenomena are to be considered discourse phenomena as in Chomsky (1976, 1977, 1978). In the combination of sentences that form discourse compounds, we can observe information forces arising from changes in the arrangements of some parts of sentences. Among such phenomena are elliptical sentences, gaps, clitics and other discourse phenomena.

Bohr (1913) proposed the existence in atoms of shells occupied by a particular number of electrons; since then considerable advances have been made in understanding how energy states of atoms are related to the distribution of electrons in these shells. In the same way, syntactic patterns predictions based on the syntactic structure of a language may significantly help to analyze the relationship between sentences and the information forces required to break the bonds that are present in order to create new compounds as discourse structures. Syntactic distribution in "sentence shells" of a given language may be strictly related to the corresponding communicative patterns expressed by a sort of "periodic table" for communicative energy detection and communicative patterns recognition in each given language.

The stability of new sentence or discourse structures is best expressed in terms of the information forces and communicative energies required to break the existing bonds, forming new sentence or discourse configurations.

At that point newly formed sentence structures may be analyzed as being more or less equivalent to the original structure from which they derive in terms of both pressure and temperature, that is, both in terms of communicative energy and informative force charge.

According to a theory of bonding, the study of syntax should also extend to matters of stability and polarization in sentence and discourse dynamics.

This does not undermine but rather reinforces Chomsky's assessment of a unique formal abstract structure underlying linguistic expression in any given tongue.

Within Chomsky's framework the conditions for a sentence to be either well-formed or ill-formed are based on a model that provides evidence that the system of abstract rules and principles must somehow be represented in the mind of the language users.

Therefore, what we human beings "cognize" is a system of mentally represented rules and principles of a type which a formal generative grammar intends to characterize. What each of us cognizes is a particular grammar of a specific language and this is explained by its relation to a more abstract object, a universal grammar, which is "a unified system of principles with a fairly rich deductive structure and some open parameters to be set by experience".

Universal Grammar provides the basis from which knowledge of a specific grammar develops. Universal Grammar can be thought of as a characterization not of human language but of the nature of the language faculty.

Universal Grammar as a biological endowment is an element of the human genotype and exposure is linked to innate properties.

What is underlined in Chomsky's framework is a biologically oriented perspective on language as a "living" system. Language is thought of as an organic system undergoing a set of transformations of different kinds.

As we all know both physics and chemistry are completely compatible with biology; they are merely acting at another level of analysis.

Similarly, it is legitimate to think of the chemical composition of biological structures as merely using a different framework.

This is how the CPP-TRS model differs from and complements the Chomskian model — it merely acts at a different level of analysis.

One more aspect needs to be underlined: within the newly established physical framework of language, textual phenomena can be analyzed to have their occurrence in natural language (CPP-TRS Text Theory of Comprehension) just like organic structures.

Further, textual phenomena can be created and produced by a "synthesis process" which I have named "text-compression" as a kind of "inorganic compound structure".

The CPP-TRS Theory of Text Comprehension deals with natural language organic phenomena, whereas the CPP-TRS Theory of Text Compression deals with textual inorganic phenomena, which are derived from organic ones.

This is a complete revolution in thinking about natural language compounds and about artificially recreated, naturally based textual phenomena.

I assume full responsibility for this discovery as well as for its practical implications and possible applications.

A descriptive, explanatory and prescriptive theory of language

The nature of the CPP-TRS Theory of Text Comprehension is that it describes and categorizes a whole set of textual phenomena, as well as explaining it in the sense that it can justify the occurrence of new phenomena by referring to the same well-defined system of representation.

The CPP-TRS Theory of Text Comprehension is descriptive in the sense that it embraces an infinite set of phenomena that can be subsumed under the CPP-TRS framework, but it is essentially explanatory.

The CPP-TRS Theory of Text Comprehension is abstract enough to achieve a deep level of explanation and is able to relate phenomena that may appear unrelated.

Let us now see if in some sense it can also be considered a generative mechanism based on a commonly shared interpretative system.

If there is a basic need to explain and justify the variety of textual phenomena that occurs in different languages and in different communicative contexts, then the CPP-TRS component will work with a UG component and a KR component.

Given the complexity of the task, it is only through a synchronous and harmonious interaction among the three that a generative model could be considered.

A whole area of research is developing to determine a predictability spectrum that explores the relationship between communicative energy and information forces in each language.

It is very important to create a system of expectations about communicative patterns and textual forms in the different languages.

In discussing the concept of prescriptive theory, I would like to point out that there is a fundamental and substantial difference between the CPP-TRS Theory of Text Comprehension and the CPP-TRS Theory of Text Compression.

The CPP-TRS based new way for consistently integrating natural language as to higher communicative value of text, based on explicating communicative function, communicative intention and communicative turn-taking visually, is actually a high transparency support based on a simple, consistent and consensual system, which directly refers to cognitive processes by reflecting them into their corresponding communicative patterns.

As in vision, texts may be recognized using communicative patterns recognition, and as in music text may be played by identifying the signs and symbols in the textual pentagram.

To "comprehend" means to "understand thoroughly" and in, literary sense, to "include".

Both definitions may be used to suggest that a theory of text understanding must be both accurate and precise, based as it is on very specific criteria that include various possibilities of actualization.

This is why the CPP-TRS Theory of Text Comprehension (Tonfoni 1989-94) has been conceived both as a new way to describe and visualize invisible aspects of natural language that are relevant to text processing and as a set of very precise techniques to be used in a way that is consistent with what they represent.

The distinction I made earlier between globally and locally controlled sequences within a text has led me to the definition of textual segments that result from a CPP-TRS based interpretation of a naturally occurring, organic text.

I want to point out that no explicit definition is being made at this level of analysis between spoken and written text, but a written text may result from adjustments that are not usually present in spoken text.

The study of textual segments is, of course, made possible through the introduction of the CPP-TRS system of signs and symbols.

Such a system works not only as an annotation device but essentially constitutes a system for detection, based on analytical techniques that can be thought of as a sort of textual spectroscopy and textual chromatography.

Identification and understanding of textual segments is based on knowledge of the structure of sentences, discourse and text according to some predictable communicative patterns. All organic text segments show basic structural features that can be perceived and recognized.

Such observations about the nature of the CPP-TRS Theory of Text Comprehension will change dramatically when we consider and analyze inorganic text structures that are made possible within the CPP-TRS Theory of Text Compression.

Text compression

As I have already shown, the CPP-TRS based Theory of Text Comprehension provides an accurate and articulated framework for attributing qualitative interpretation to a text globally or to text segments locally and is therefore a useful model for representing text execution at both levels.

We now describe the CPP-TRS based Theory of Text Compression.

"To compress" means literally "to press together and force into less space"; a compressed text is a text in which information density is being reorganized not just quantitatively but qualitatively with a multilayered distribution and in a different textual space.

The difference between a quantitative and a qualitative approach to information density in text and text segments can only be conceived within a Quantum Theory of Language based on qualitative reasoning about communication.

CPP-TRS is a model for text execution and, according to a set of interpretative cues, it is a qualitative model that generates a model of text that is ready to be interpreted and executed by explicating visually qualitative information about each text unit, as can be seen in Schemes 1 and 2:

By text unit I mean a further step in CPP-TRS text processing, where not only local and global control interpretive cues have been identified as in text and text segments annotation, but where an adjustment has also taken place involving the temperature-pressure relationship and balancing.

A text unit is the first step for inorganic text production and is aimed at reducing the natural distance between text producer and text perceiver through the use of interpretation cues. The CPP-TRS Theory of Text Compression aims to reduce the distance by significantly shortening the existing bandwidth in current interaction and by keeping the interpretation cues transparent.

Therefore, a CPP-TRS based model for text compression does not operate directly from

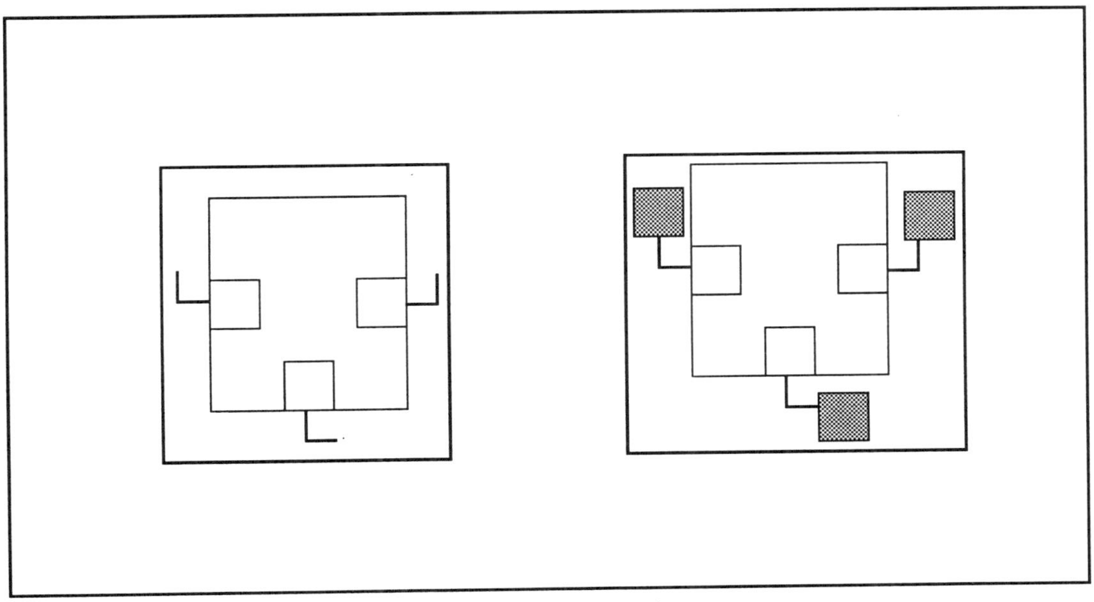

Scheme 1. *Scheme 2.*

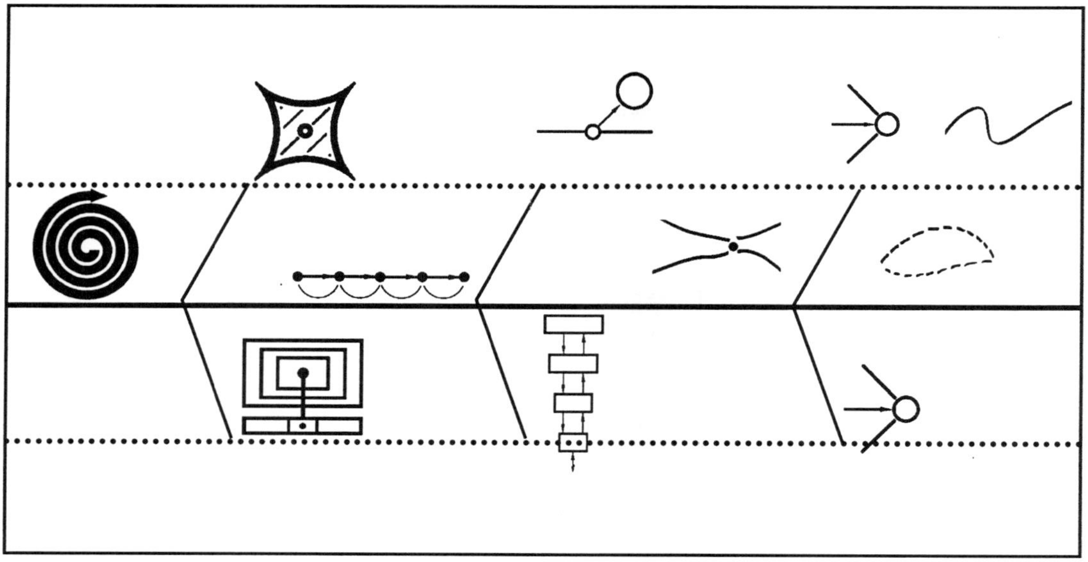

Scheme 3.

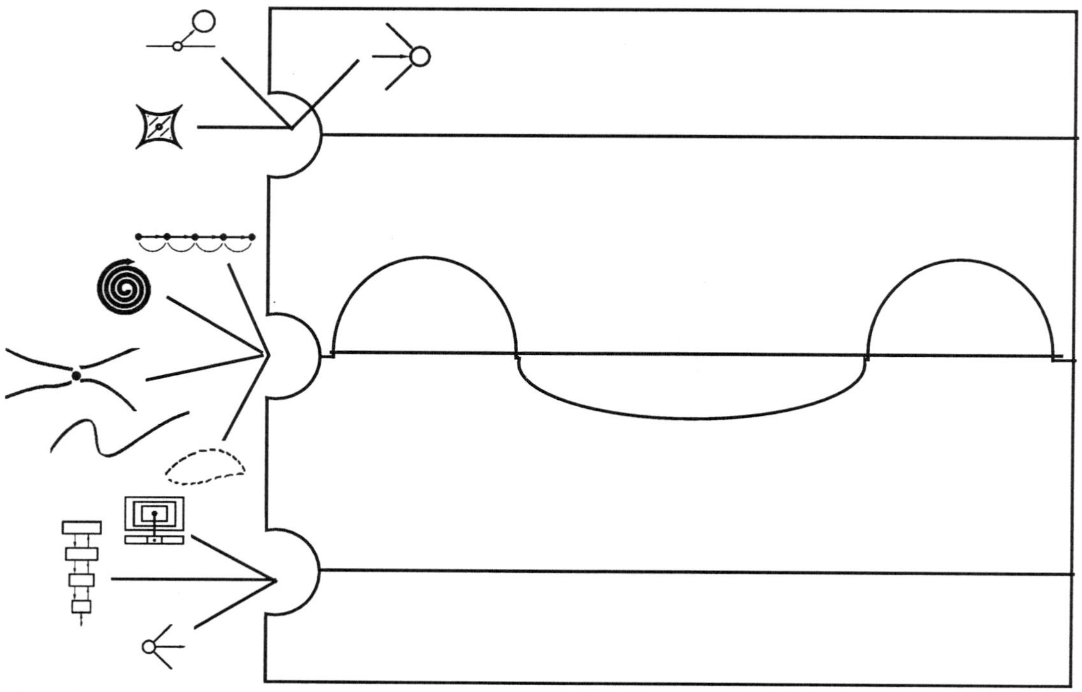

Scheme 4

texts, only from a CPP-TRS processed text that shows qualitative information about text execution through a consistent application of signs and symbols.

Signs controlling text globally do not have to undergo any further change during text compression. Symbols controlling text locally will activate a further process, which I have named multilayered distribution of text segments.

In order to understand what this process consists of let us now have a look at the following Scheme 3, which represents a High Compression Device for text segments multilayered distribution:

As a consequence of three-layered distribution each text is configurated according to a dynamic process, which will visually and consistently represent the quality of information. A CPP-TRS processed text which undergoes a process of text compression, will look like the illustration in Scheme 4:

The three-layered distribution of text segments according to the local control symbol is in fact a reduction of a ten-layered distribution.

The upper level corresponds to those local control symbols representing a lower density of information; the intermediate level corresponds to those local control symbols that represent a medium density of information; and the lower level corresponds to those local control symbols which represent a high level density of information.

By checking the measure of the circles, the exact symbol can be detected by the use of a Textual Template.

Qualitative Compression is the result of a very accurate process of information packaging based on inorganic textual configurations, which I have defined as CPTRU, Communicatively Positioned Textually Represented Unit.

CPTRU configurations are topic-driven and constitute CPTRU territories, which are qualitatively and quantitatively different from the text from which they are derived.

The process each CPTRU has undergone is visible both at the level of global control signs (textual mask) and at the level of local control symbols (textual template).

The access to global information is the first step in CPTRU territories visualization; access to local information is regulated by a further level of visualization (textual template).

Once information is compressed, which means that it has undergone major structural changes, the CPP-TRS framework allows for visibility of the processes. In other words, any text and text segment undergoing a compression process will keep visible traces of what has happened to it.

Any decision to promote transparency in communication has been maintained at every step, including the planning of a transparent mechanism both for quantitative and qualitative text compression.

It should also be pointed out here that text compression applies to natural language.

Such processes cannot be transported to either visual or gestural states of information; they radically differ in their properties and characterization.

α, β, γ radioactive information territories

A processed text unit that acquires a high level of communicative visibility becomes an inorganic structure aimed at increasing the effectiveness of communicative processes and intercourses by reducing the bandwidth between text producer and text perceiver.

A CPTRU structure is therefore an extremely powerful unit both for information and communication visibility.

Any CPTRU structure is indexed, stored and retrieved, based on a topic or keyword identification.

Some topic driven CPTRU structures constitute information territories.

The exploration of information territories is very important in order to detect the different amounts of qualitative information that are presented about a certain topic.

Inorganic CPTRU structures may undergo further processes, which we will now consider.

Transformational processes that occur on a CPTRU structure level may modify the communicative energy value and the information force value as well as different levels, including radical changes.

This is why I have postulated a kernel theory of communicative energy transformation and identified three different kinds of radiations that may be active on CPTRU, each modifying it more or less radically. I have named them α, β, γ radiation in close analogy with the radiation found, analyzed and reproduced in nuclear energy phenomena.

These kinds of radiation apply to CPTRU structures at different levels and produce qualitatively different kinds of reactions. Just as in nuclear physics, they perform on a qualitatively different level. Let us now analyze them:

α radiation applies first to topic-driven CPTRU territories and then to sign-controlled CPTRU.

When applied to a topic, it will enlighten, that is, activate a certain CPTRU topic-driven territory and will aggregate according to the communicative patterns configuration assigned.

Here is an example of aggregation:

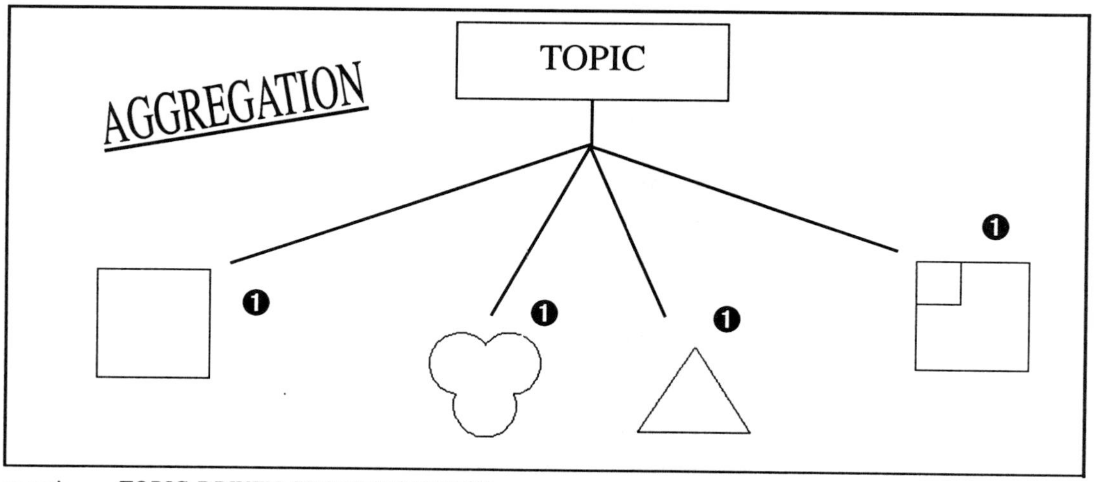

α active on TOPIC-DRIVEN CPTRU TERRITORY

α radiation will then apply to sign-driven CPTRU, triggering attraction among the same sign-driven CPTRU.

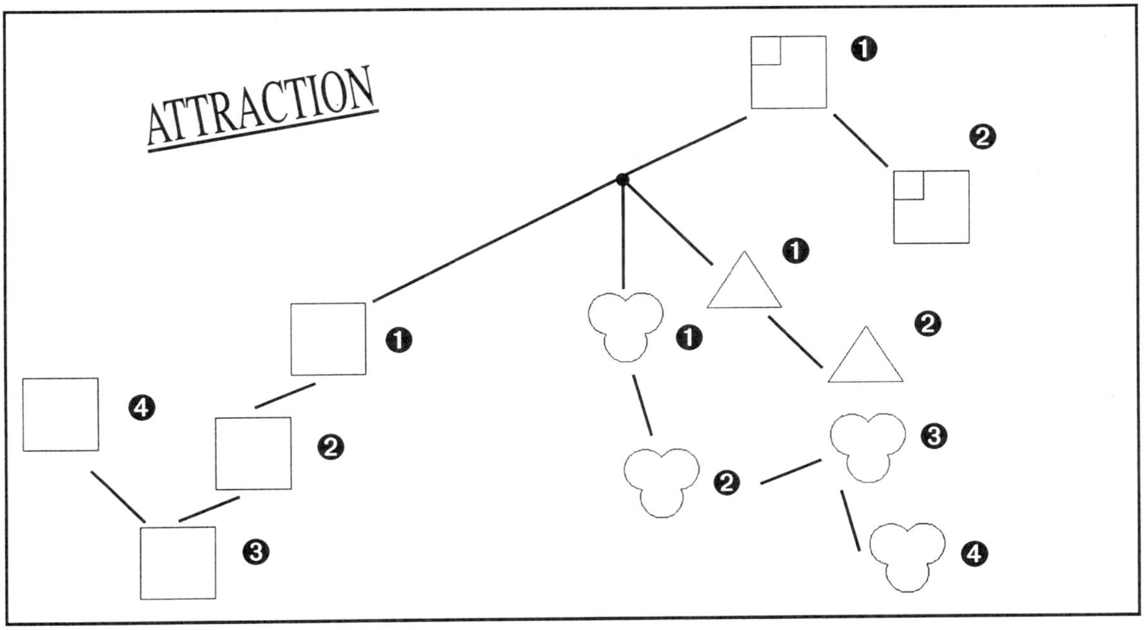

α active on SIGN DRIVEN CPTRU

α radiation produces acceleration, but cannot create transformation because both topic and sign represent a stable component that does not allow any change at the core that may affect the CPTRU structure.

Nevertheless α is able to activate, aggregate and attract; thus it can be defined as that kind of radiation that may produce acceleration but no transformation; α-active CPTRU structures may aggregate and attract.

γ radiation applies to the kernel of a CPTRU. It can activate and excite a specific locally controlled textual segment (or set of segments) that is symbol driven. Thus it is able to trigger a reaction. Such a result may be defined as a transformation because it may completely alter the qualitative nature of the symbol driven textual segment (or segments).

Both new and transformed segments must keep a visible trace of the reactions they have been undergoing (See *γ Active* , page 44).

A γ-driven transformation implies total access to and visibility of local information structures, that is the information kernel, at a deep level, differently from α. A γ-driven transformation carries instructions about the specific kind of transformation occurring. The excited CPTRU will therefore retain its original state as well as the transformed one (trace). To conclude, γ radiation is able to produce excitation and transformation by leaving a trace but no acceleration. It applies to symbol-controlled text segments, that represent the unstable component.

When γ active CPTRU is excited and keeps a trace, α radiation will necessarily be active as well.

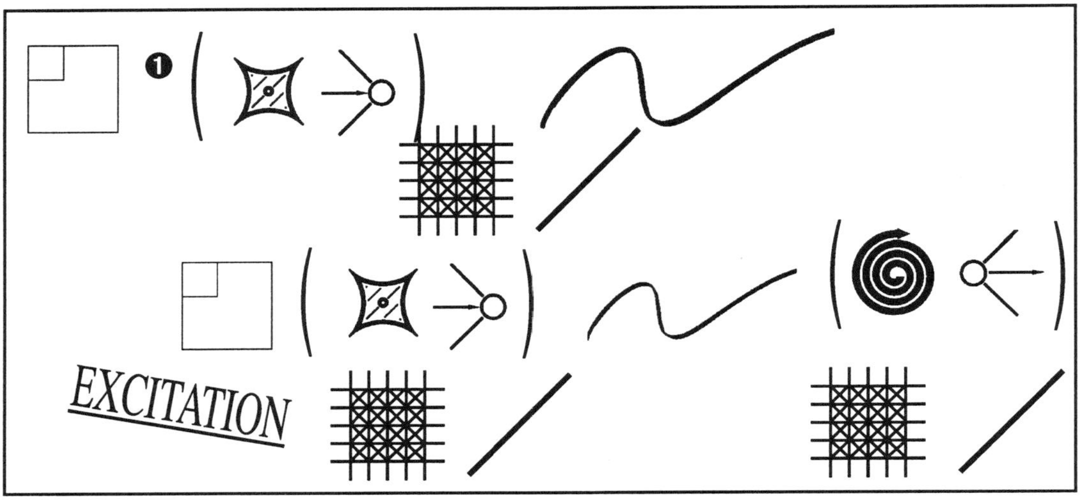

γ Active.

β radiation has been left to the last as it is the most powerful and radical of the three kinds of radiation.

β radiation applies to the kernel of a CPTRU with consequences and side-effects for the overall system; it activates, excites and explodes many or all locally controlled text segments that are symbol-driven. It is therefore able to trigger a very powerful reaction, the strongest one among those we have considered. This is a transformation because it completely alters the qualitative nature of the identified symbol driven-text segment (or segments).

As in earlier examples, both new and transformed text segment (or segments) will retain a trace of the reaction. Consider the β active example.

An active β implies that α and γ are active as well and it causes very strong side effects.

If β applies to larger text segments it may alter the qualitative nature of the whole CPTRU to a point where even the more stable component, which is sign-driven, may actually disintegrate. A high level of control therefore needs to be kept on the changes made.

If γ radiation is very strong, it may produce a high level explosion causing α and β to be active to a point where they produce both transformation and acceleration.

In such case acceleration is produced as a consequence of a strong α activation to cope with the radiation of γ activated by β. As in γ, any β-driven transformation implies total access and visibility of local information structures at a deep level.

β radiation is able to produce excitation, explosion and transformation by leaving a trace and may also trigger α into producing acceleration as well.

This applies to turn-taking symbols controlled text segments, which are linked to local control symbols and together represent the unstable component of CPTRU.

To conclude, β radiation always triggers transformation and may sometimes produce acceleration as well.

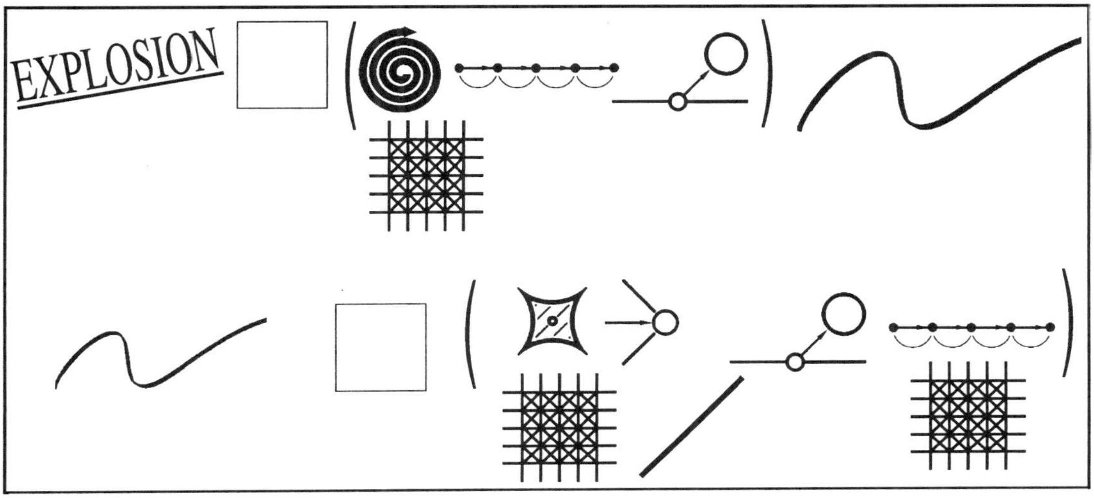

β Active

A β active CPTRU, while exploding, will activate γ and α as well as retain a trace.

The kind of phenomena I have described are the result of operations that need to be controlled each time. They can be of tremendous help in raising transparency in communication.

This is just like X-raying texts to facilitate dramatically information exchange based on a shared reference system for interpretation.

Amplifying perception, and amplifying technology

Creating a theory intended to produce a consistent set of practical models and evolving it to a point where completely new scenarios are made visible, entails not merely the possibility of using new and powerful interpretive tools but also the configuration of new devices and machines to perform known operations in a new and much more effective way.

An artificial system may be based on analysis and reproduction of an observed natural system, which retains its own limitations, or it may be derived from a model evolved from a natural system.

A system of artificial vision may be based on the analysis of the natural human visual system with all its limitations or be based on an optimized model of vision that overcomes these limitations.

Human vision depends on many structural facts. There are inhibitory processes, accommodation processes, visual acuity and different levels of adaptation.

To give an example of an active inhibitory process, we can think of the phenomenon of simultaneous contrast, where a patch of light appears to be much darker when it is surrounded by a bright background than when set against a black one. This is due to the inhibitory effect of the surrounding retina on the central region, induced by the bright surround. Many colour contrast phenomena are similarly caused.

For example, if a blue light is projected onto a large white screen, the white screen appears yellow. The blue stimulus falling on the central retina causes inhibition of blue sensibility in the periphery, hence the white background appears to be lacking its blue light. The same thing happens in communication and information processing.

I have distinguished two qualitatively different kinds of inhibitory processes: script-driven and cognitive-driven inhibitory processes.

An individual's script based reasoning may inhibit new processing and undermine knowledge. As Schank (1988) has pointed out, people tend to keep their scripts and it takes some effort and energy on their part to revise and update them. They are not always willing to do this and either consciously or unconsciously resist.

Because of cognitive capability driven inhibitory processes, individuals may find difficulties in processing texts that have either too high or too low an information density. I have discovered phenomena of spacial summation and temporal summation occurring in text understanding as well.

In other words, in spacial summation two qualitatively different kinds of textual information add their perceptive effects so that while either one alone may be inadequate to foster understanding, when presented simultaneously they may do so.

In temporal summation, two textual stimuli (which may just be words) even if each is weak, may cause understanding if presented in rapid succession within the same text.

Temporal summation is consistent with a quantum theory of language; it has been shown that fluctuations in the number of quanta in a text are responsible for the varied levels of understanding; increasing the duration of a textual stimulus increases the probability of text perception.

I have mentioned only a few phenomena that occur in so-called natural text perception. There are many more to be considered and taken into account when planning new communication technology that should aim to amplify real human capabilities.

By assuming such a perspective, which is based on the earlier assumption that any new technology should amplify and expand the potential of naturally working systems, I here introduce three applications based on this as a practical example of a design of a CPP-TRS technology, starting from an optimized natural model, in which the bugs and limitation that were part of the original model have been identified.

A technology that has a bug is dangerous, because this bug will be magnified and proliferate.

Let us start by considering the commercial application of heat or infra-red copying methods, thermography.

"What happens in thermography is that a special kind of copy paper and the original copy are placed in contact with each other and run through a machine where they are exposed to infra-red or heat rays.

"The original copy absorbs the rays in areas darkened by print, line drawings or other illustrations, making the same impressions on the heat sensitive surface of the copy paper. The original with the new copy paper attached may be put through the machine repeatedly to produce the number of copies desired" (literal definition of Thermography in the *Encyclopaedia Britannica*).

This is the existing machine: what I have designed is an amplifier copying machine, where the original copy both undergoes a process of compression and possibly allows radiation in order to produce multiple audience, multiple target texts. This will only be possible through an accurate and consistent application of CPP-TRS scanning, CPTRU information territories definition and α, β, γ radiation.

Such a tool will allow control of each set of operations performed on the text, resulting in a powerful transparency promoting amplifier technology.

Let us now consider another popular machine, the fax. "In facsimile reproducing processes, a transmitter scans the original material, converting the image into electrical signals that are sent over telephone lines or by other means of communication, such as radio or microwave. A receiver reconverts the signals into the original image on paper" (literal definition of Facsimile in the *Encyclopaedia Britannica*).

This is the existing machine: what I have designed is an amplified facsimile, where the text with the CPP- TRS annotation is sent out to facilitate translation processes based on the fact that the content is organized in such way as to make visible the qualitative interpretation of each outgoing text.

Other kinds of operations may be explained as a set of instructions for specific reformulation of precisely defined text segments.

These are just some examples I have introduced to provide evidence about the concept of an amplifier technology based on raising individuals' control and their monitoring of communication and information processes.

Part Three
Introduction to Quantum Theory of Language

CPP-TRS: A Universal Grammar of Linguistic Performance

Introduction

In this chapter a new framework is presented. CPP-TRS (Tonfoni, 1989-94) is both a new model for reframing a theory of language performance as communicative action and a methodology based on a set of clearly defined conceptual tools.

CPP-TRS also constitutes a visual language by itself, based on a set of highly articulated and consistently combinable visual elements, which are effective and practical devices for representing communicative actions.

CPP-TRS is based on a radical assumption: there is a set of universally valid categories that play a crucial role in linguistic performance; universal categories in language are not just to be found at the syntactic level, they can be found at the pragmatic level as well, Pragmatics must be scientifically grounded and may be defined as the realm of "competence of performance".

In CPP-TRS a text can be defined as the basic communicative active linguistic entity and a new terminology is carefully introduced or redefined to ensure that new definitions will not carry old meanings and that redefined terminology will not cause any ambiguity. It is therefore important that new concepts such as Communicative Positioning Program are carefully explained, redefined and reframed, and that existing concepts such as linguistic performance are analyzed and described so they can be agreed and mutually shared concepts and practical interpretative tools.

CPP-TRS: A New Framework

In order to explain why a paradigm that is explicitly intended to address old questions and solve old problems in new ways is both consistent and really new, it is very important to make sure that definitions and terms are mutually understood. First, let us go back to the difference between "competence" and "performance" (Chomsky, 1957, 1965). Let us add that a CPP-TRS based perspective on language as communicative action attempts both to describe and explain what a competent performance is. In Chomsky (1965) competence is "the speaker's-hearer's knowledge of the language" contrasted with performance, which is "the actual use of language in concrete situations". What needs to be added, however, is that the present approach to performance needs to be scientific and rigorous; not merely observation driven, but explanatory and predictive as well.

A CPP-TRS approach differs from others primarily because of the basic problems it considers relevant. These may be synthesized in the following way:

There is something innate in language that is found not solely at the syntactic level but also at the pragmatic level. There is a universally valid set of rules but these are not merely syntactic rules. They are also communicative positioning attitudes that we can find in any language. They work on top of the different languages and all languages reflect them in a way that is so consistent that they may be recognized, in spite of the differences among languages and the various culture-specific components, by language-dependent patterns that allow native speakers to recognize them.

There are universal categories, like syntactic categories, which are defined as communicative positioning attitudes, that are consistently reflected in texts and text segments in the form of communicative patterns, so that the native speaker may recognize them as active either on a global or a local level.

The basic entity for communicative positioning detection and identification is not the sentence but the text, which is redefined as the basic communicative positioned entity. Text segments may show an alternation of different communicative positioning attitudes.

People have an innate capacity to recognize what is well formed and ill formed, not just at the level of the sentence, but also at the level of text and text segment, both globally and locally.

Native speakers have a particular competence for deciding whether a sentence is acceptable, correct or incorrect; but a communicative actor also has a competence to decide whether a text or a text segment is consistent with its respective communicative positioning attitude, both globally and locally.

"Rule governed creativity" not only justifies the infinite number of sentences as the output of a definite set of rules, but also justifies an unlimited set of texts, which consistently represent a limited set of communicative positioning attitudes.

Speakers have innate competence and capacity to produce and interpret an infinite number of sentences, to evaluate their syntactic correctness and to notice special relationships between them (such as an active versus a passive sentence), but the communicative actor also is competent to perceive an infinite number of texts and text segments and evaluate them against their respective communicative positions globally and locally and to note special relationships between some of them (as in the case of informative versus explanatory texts, and analytical vs synthetical text segments).

Both introspection and observation of syntactic phenomena are needed as well as self-reflection on one's own communicative positioning and cognitive awareness of other individuals' communicative positioning, in order to ensure a theory of communication works consistently.

If we consider the notion of 'correctness', we can see it as dependent on syntactic criteria, syntactic criteria being part of a biologically determined and innate background of knowledge (Chomsky, 1957, 1965).

In CPP-TRS (Tonfoni, 1989-94) the notion of 'correctness' is redefined in terms of consistency and is related to cognitive criteria, given a certain set of communicative attitudes that are part of a biologically determined cognitive programme. We can thus say that communicative positioning attitudes are consistent with the cognitive programme each individual has biologically. We can also add that the result of a certain communicative positioning attitude or attitudes needs to be consistent, in the sense of adhering to such an attitude or attitudes as shown in the result, that is, in texts and text segments. If there is a discrepancy between the communicative positioning attitude intended and its reflection on texts and text segments, then problems in interpretation and actual understanding may occur.

The "competence of performance" shown by a communicative actor should prevent such discrepancy from occurring, unless it is intentional. Some discrepancy may occur if an actor is being uncooperative.

As communication is based on cooperation and mutual sharing of an agreed and accepted system, a discrepancy between a communicative positioning attitude and its reflection on a text or a text segment can be viewed like a syntactic rule and its violation in a certain sentence. If a native speaker is able, based on his competence in his native language, to recognize, name and categorize different elements of a sentence as subject or article or verb, noun phrase and verb phrase, the same individual should be able to recognize, name and categorize differently positioned texts and text segments as representing differing positioning attitudes, both globally and locally. Just as transformations occur when applying the system of syntactic rules (Chomsky, 1957), parts of the same text may undergo a set of transformations on both a local and a global level (Tonfoni, 1989-94, 1995).

Consistency between the Communicative Positioning Level and the respective Text Representation Level, both locally and globally, is what matters to ensure that the text may be processed as it was intended, consistency being the result of matching. A text may then be defined as consistent within itself, holding together and retaining form, as a result of this. The problem of inconsistency between the language output and the intention has been discussed many times in linguistics (Austin, 1962; Searle, 1968). The Speech Act theory (Searle, 1968) identifies a set of verbal categories representing intentions.

In CPP-TRS some specific terms and verbs have been technically redefined to represent specific communicative intentions and have been turned into interpretative categories which apply to text and texts segments, thereby being active on both a global and a local level. Defining precisely what a certain communicative positioning attitude entails or implies is of extreme relevance so as not to expand the number of categories to the extent that the system becomes unmanageable and ineffective. On the other hand, it is important to make sure that each of the categories covers all the varieties of text occurrences, which are unlimited.

This is exactly what happens in syntax: the selected categories need to be adequate and sufficient to cover all possible sentence outputs. The numbers need to be restricted, otherwise the system becomes unmanageable.

What is meant by being cognitively bound is the common basis of a cognitive programme, that allows an individual to recognize a set of communicative positioning attitudes that may generate an unlimited set of text occurrences. What is meant by culturally bound, on the other hand, is a common set of assumptions and beliefs from a certain culture which reflect a set of agreed and context-sensitive rules, that allow any individual in the group to trace back a certain communicative behaviour to its original causes.

These two aspects, cognition and culture, are linked, but must be recognized as entirely different components working at different levels.

Research has been made into knowledge representation and how knowledge is organized around certain facts and events at various levels of complexity.

Models of knowledge organization are designed to be used for knowledge filing, retrieving and indexing, such as the Frame (Minsky, 1975), the Script (Schank, 1977), the Plan (Wilensky, 1983), and the Plot Unit (Lehnert, 1981).

All of these models address the problem of knowledge organization in certain domains and for specific purposes. Analyzing culturally bound communicative behaviours implies observation and knowledge acquisition about facts and events. Cognitively bound communicative attitudes require self-reflection and cognitive awareness. Self-reflection is intended to observe self-activated cognitive processes, communicative positioning attitudes and the way they reflect on text or text segments. Cognitive awareness, as a result of self-reflection, is the capacity to recognize other individuals communicative positioning attitudes from the way they are reflected on texts or text segments.

In order to proceed scientifically in a realm where many components are invisible as in the realm of language and communication, an important step, in addition to the accurate definition of terms, is visualization. Visualizing invisible processes or elements is a tremendous support for self-observation and cognitive awareness. If the model is cognitively consistent, it will be used in and for any language.

CPP-TRS, being a cognitively consistent methodology, can be used in any language in the sense that the same invisible aspects and processes are active in all languages and CPP-TRS may help them surface by defining them and giving them a visual representation.

In CPP-TRS communicative positioning attitudes have been defined carefully by giving a specific meaning to a set of ordinary terms, turning them into technically defined terms.

Each of the terms has an equivalent visual representation, which can be substituted and used to represent visually what the term means. This is why CPP-TRS (Tonfoni, 1989-94) is based on a precise terminology (which carries its own visual representation, articulated into visual dynamic schemes, textual machines and textual canvases, in order to represent the deep structure of text) and a set of icons (articulated into global signs, local symbols and turn-taking symbols that represent the output text surface).

Since CPP-TRS is a cognitively consistent visual language, it can be used for any language in the sense that those invisible aspects and processes which constitute the communicative positioning of a text may be visually integrated within the text itself. Visualizing, defining and creating articulated metaphors to explain complex phenomena or processes which cannot be seen is often practised in a scientific framework.

In *The Society of the Mind* (Minsky, 1986) the metaphor of a society is used to represent the functioning of the mind in its various components. Some new terminology is introduced as well, but it is largely a set of redefined terms that constitute the explanatory kernel of the theory.

CPP-TRS (Tonfoni, 1989-94) is intended to define a Universal Grammar of Communicative Positioning Actions, which constitutes the Core Grammar of a Competence of Performance. In order to be considered as scientifically grounded, a theory of language should entail observation, explanation, description and definition in order to make predictions and evaluations based on a set of clearly identified criteria.

The explanatory component in CPP-TRS addresses the issue of identifying, defining and categorizing basic underlying processes which are the basis of any communicative positioning attitude. They correspond to the global and overall planning of communicative actions to be taken. They are active at a "deep structure" level of text; they work at a global level and are subject to change, movement and transformation. For exactly these reasons, I have chosen a set of visual and dynamic schemes to represent them in action: textual canvases and textual machines.

Deep Structure Of Texture

A "canvas", redefined as a metaphor, is a defined territory to be progressively organized both globally and locally. A textual canvas represents an overall "deep structure" for an identified communicative plan to be worked out in detail according to different communicative positioning patterns, that will be chosen later.

A "machine" refers to a "device for energy transformation and transmission".

Textual machines are physical models of processes that cannot be represented in words alone. They are devices for observing and defining that which, until now, has not been observed or defined.

Textual machines are intended to represent visually, physically and dynamically global and local transformations and transmission of communicative energy at a "deep structure" level.

Textual Canvases and Textual Machines in CPP-TRS (Tonfoni, 1989-94) are intimately connected in that they both relate to the "deep structure". As such, they are extremely useful tools for self-reflection and self-observation (*More information about each of my CPP-TRS visual tools can be found in the summarized English version of my three Italian books, which has been published with the title* Writing as a Visual Art *[with J. Richardson and with Marvin Minsky's foreword], Intellect Books, 1994*).

Let us now present textual canvases and textual machines and their respective links. Textual canvases are dynamic visual schemes to be used in practical ways to integrate text production. Textual machines, on the other hand, are interpretation devices intended to explain, not to produce text.

– Textual Canvases

a. Density in Texture — This canvas shows the different possible densities of information to be organized and turned into a text,

b. Word Explosion and Word Chaining — This canvas represents the cognitive process of free association triggered by a word. It also depicts how a group of words can be linked together from a word explosion so that they form a logical, linear chain. The word chain that results from this process will first be a sentence but can also be extended to a set of sentences and paragraphs.

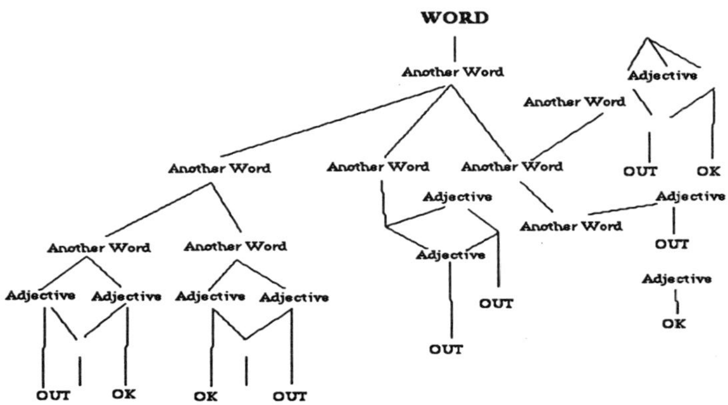

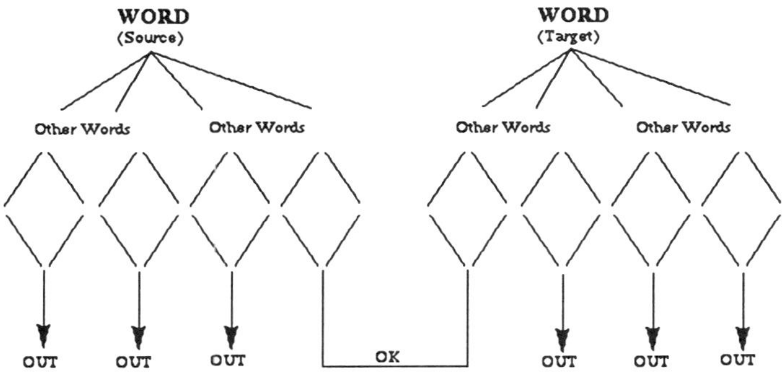

c. Metaphor Creation — This canvas illustrates that a metaphor begins with two word explosions: one for the source word and one for the target word. The source word is the word we start with, and the target word is one that has been chosen for transferring a new meaning to the source word.

d. Pattern Recognition and Analogies in Stories — This canvas shows how a visual frame may represent the logical structure of a story at a conceptual level. Once a story is visually represented, it becomes easy to replicate its structural patterns to create other conceptually analogous stories.

e. Global Narrative Text Planning — This canvas represents a visual scheme for globally planning narrative text. A canvas such as this enables us visually to represent a long story that may encompass a number of events, protagonists and possible outcomes. It opens up the possibility of conceiving many different ways to develop the story while retaining and checking its coherence.

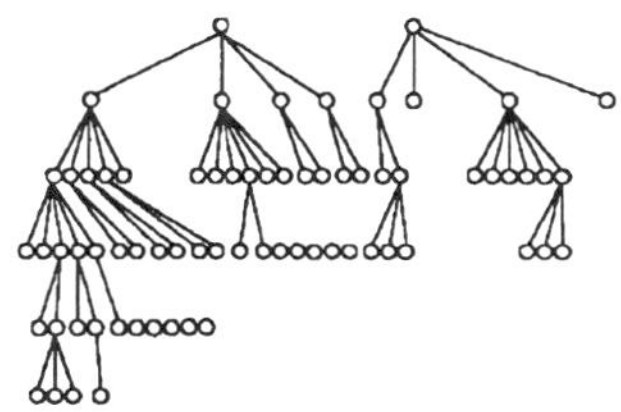

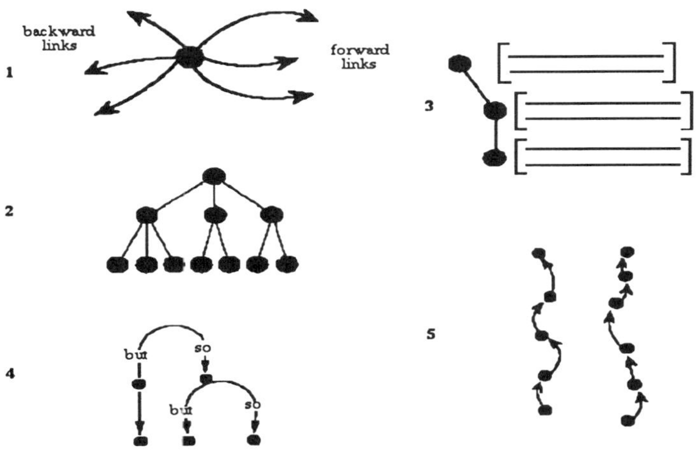

f. Local Narrative Text Planning — This five-part canvas helps us visualize the details of a narrative text. It visually represents how to examine the backward and forward links from a narrative concept, to visualize a story in different ways from a particular point, to use temporal and causal connectors to link narrative concepts, and to reconstruct the story differently by changing its sequence.

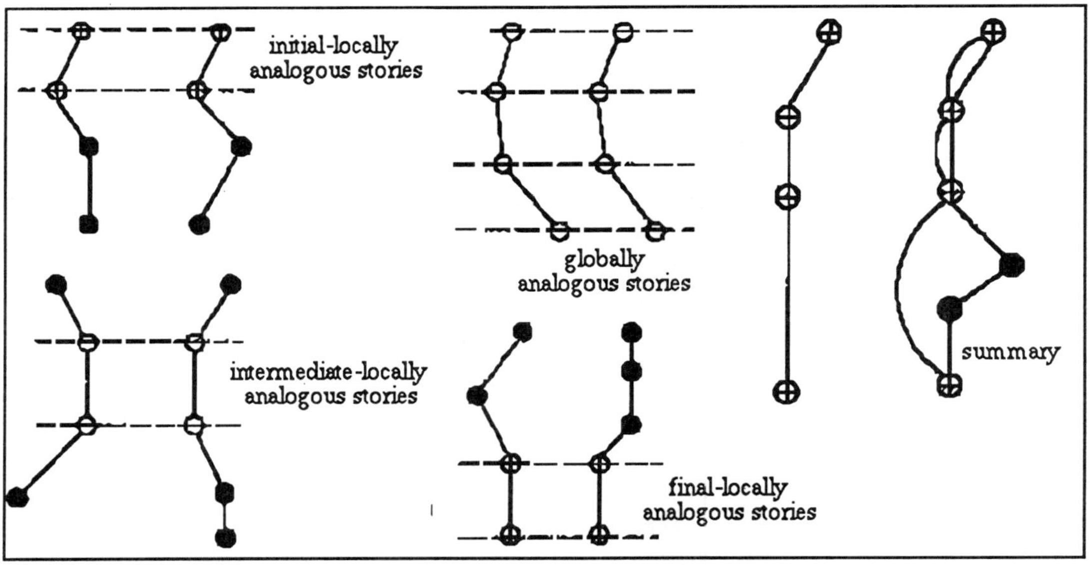

g. Analogous Story Planning — This canvas is a visual aid for planning or finding other stories that are analogous to a particular story. It visualizes the different ways that two stories are analogous. They can be partially analogous — which means they are initially, intermediately, or finally analogous — or they can be totally or globally analogous.

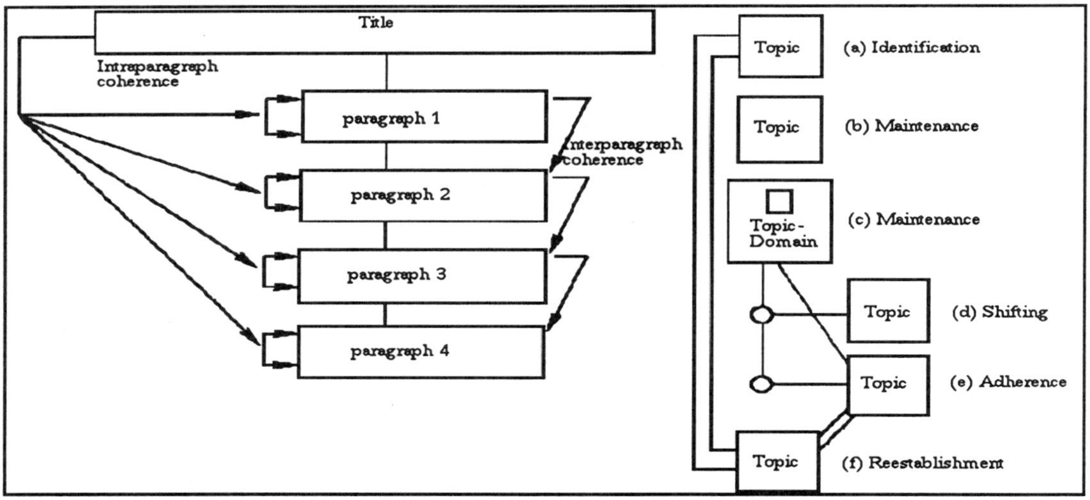

h. Explanatory Text Drawing — This canvas presents visual schemes for planning and organizing an explanatory text by exhibiting a logical progression or causal or temporal development. The first visual scheme resembles a traditional outline and shows the logical progression of the text, starting with a title and flowing down through the division and development of a set of paragraphs. The second scheme provides an alternative to the strictly logical progression of paragraphs, and instead focuses on identifying and maintaining a topic.

j. Dialogue-Conversation — This canvas is for visualizing a conversation, recording its rhythm, and tracking its evolution. It is divided by a vertical line into two parts: the left records the contributions of the initiator of the conversation, while the right records those of the addressee. The lines flowing down through the initiator's and addressee's parts trace the dynamics of the dialogue as it progresses. The process of planning and drawing a conversation on the canvas has the effect of slowing it down so that it stays focused and heads towards the same goal. It also enables a detailed, written reconstruction of the conversation.

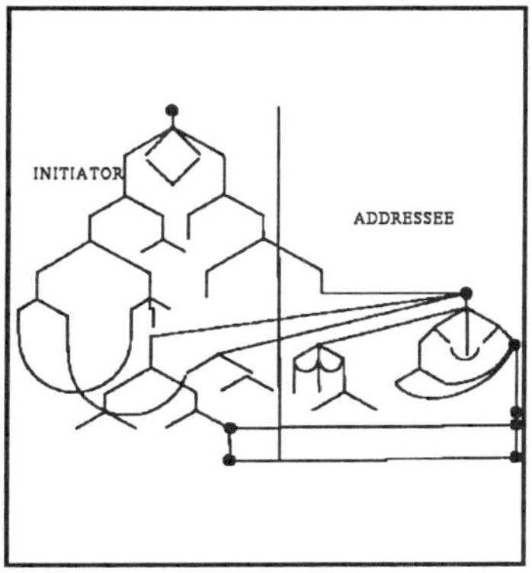

k. Collective Text Perception — This is a two-part canvas. The first part helps us to visualize a particular type of collective text planning called "collage writing". Collage writing may be done by a group of individuals who collectively endeavour to create a text by piecing together their individual written contributions. The second part of the canvas represents "mosaic reading". Mosaic reading shows how different text receivers can read the same text in different ways. In mosaic reading, a small group of people summarize the same text and then compare them to see how they differ.

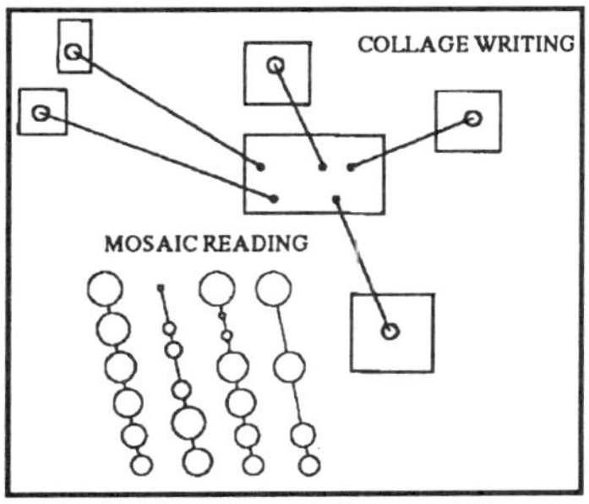

l. Text Rotation — This canvas visualizes an organization process for those texts that carry the "same" message to readers who have differing information needs and backgrounds in order to accommodate their particular perspectives and expectations.

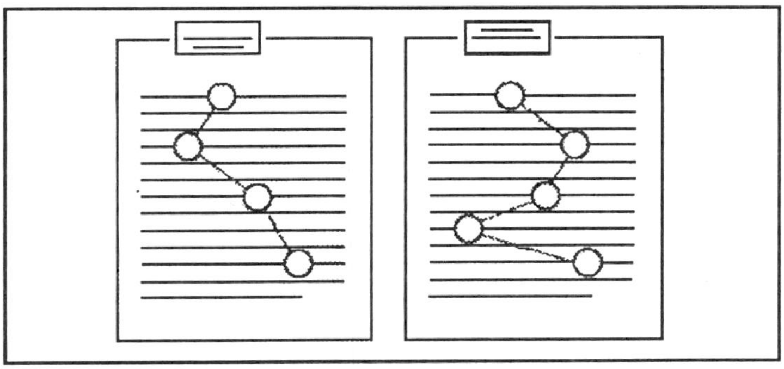

m. Hypertext — This canvas is particularly suited for "hands-on" explanatory texts such as instruction manuals or procedural guides. This is non-linear and intended to be used to fulfil differing information needs.

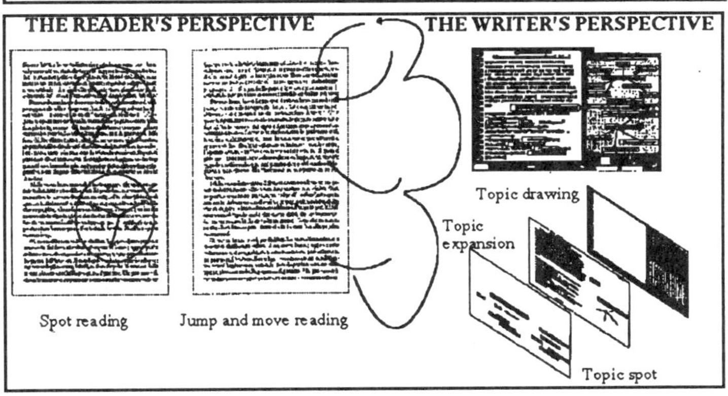

To conclude, analyzing a text or text segments is linked to the communicative framework from which text or text segments derive. This is why textual canvases should be considered not merely as practical tools but as interpretation devices for communicative positioning detection.

– Textual Machines

Textual machines are dynamic visualization tools for representing different cognitive processes active both separately and together. Let us explore their meaning.

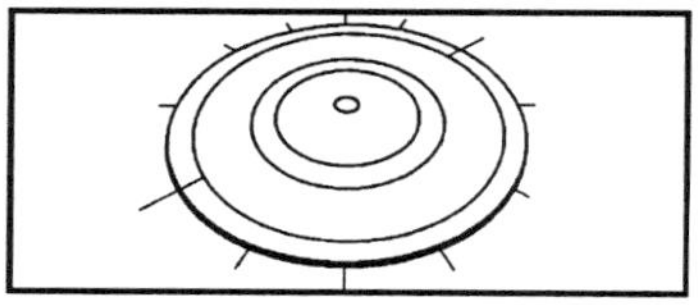

i. Machine for Simple Rotation of a Word — This machine models the cognitive process of freely associating words with one particular word. It is a three-dimensional representation of the same concept as the canvas for word explosion.

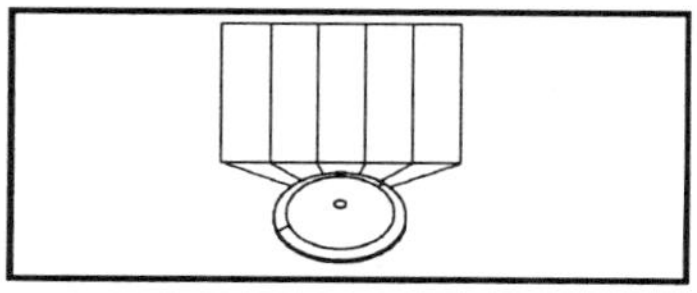

ii. Machine for Complex Rotation of a Word — This machine models the cognitive process of selecting attributes or adjectives, and then organizes them linearly. It is a three-dimensional representation of the same concept as the canvas for word-chaining.

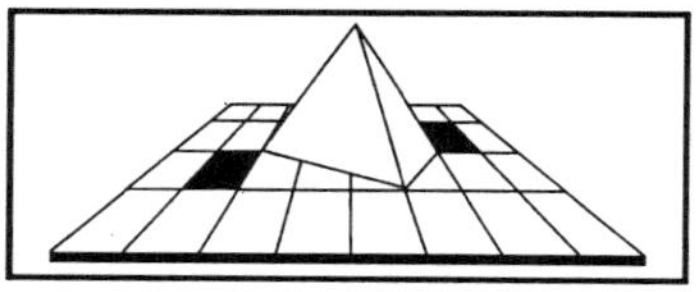

iii. Text Motion Machine — This machine provides a dynamic, three-dimensional way to think about a narrative text in which many possibilities are kept open. It is a three-dimensional representation of the same concept as the canvas for planning a narrative text.

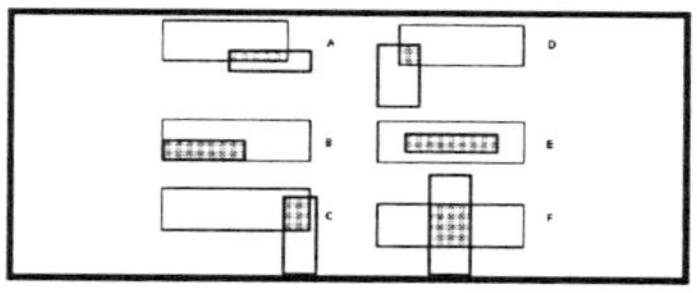

iv. Textual Lens — This machine models the cognitive processes of focusing on some part of the text and then expanding the aspect that is considered to be most relevant. It is a three-dimensional representation of the same concept as the canvas for textual rotation.

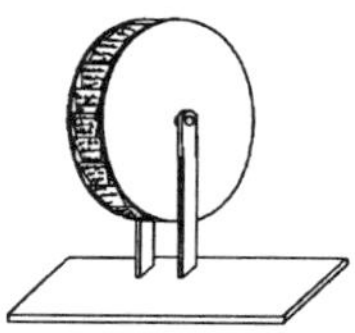

v. Wheel for Text Browsing — This machine models the way information is processed and how much the text implicitly or explicitly conveys, and how narrative text has forward and backward links. It is a three-dimensional representation of the same concept as the canvas for planning narrative text in a detailed way.

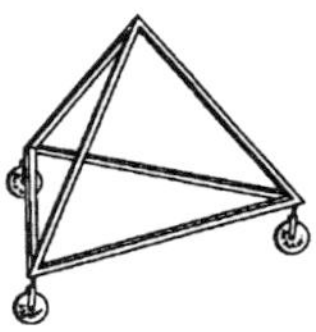

vi. Carriage for Memory Text — This machine enables us to see the relationship between an evocative word and a memorized story. It demonstrates how the same word may trigger many different stories. It is a three-dimensional representation of the same concept as the canvas for finding analogies in stories.

vii. Carriage for Explanatory Text (Simple) — This machine visualizes the process of knowledge acquisition and storage. It is a three-dimensional representation of the same concept as the canvas for planning and drawing explanatory texts.

viii. Carriage for Explanatory Text (Complex) — This machine is a more complex version of the machine above. It models the process of knowledge acquisition, storage and retrieval. It is a three-dimensional representation of the same concept as the canvas for hypertext.

ix. Three-Floor Rotation Machine for Poetry — This machine models the structuring of evocative text that triggers emotions and personal feelings. It is a three-dimensional representation of the same concept as the canvas for creating a metaphor.

ix

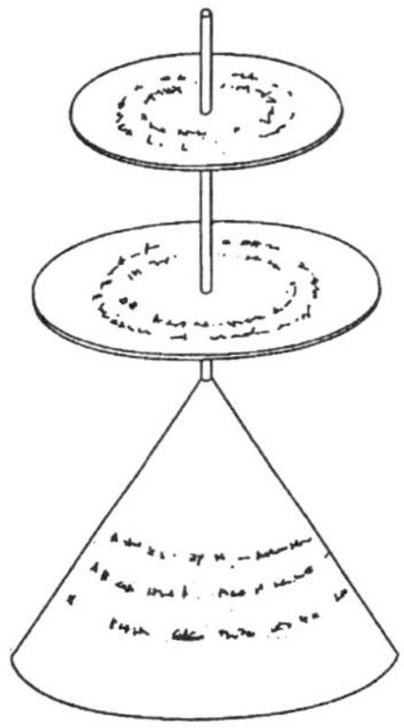

x. Machine for Transferring Text — This machine models how a text constructor can organize the same topic in two different text styles. It is a three-dimensional representation of the same concept as the canvas for organizing the density of the text.

x

xi. Device for Transforming Text in Phases — This device models the process of transforming text paragraph by paragraph from some initial version to a final version. It is a three-dimensional representation of the same concept as the canvas for organizing the density of the text.

xi

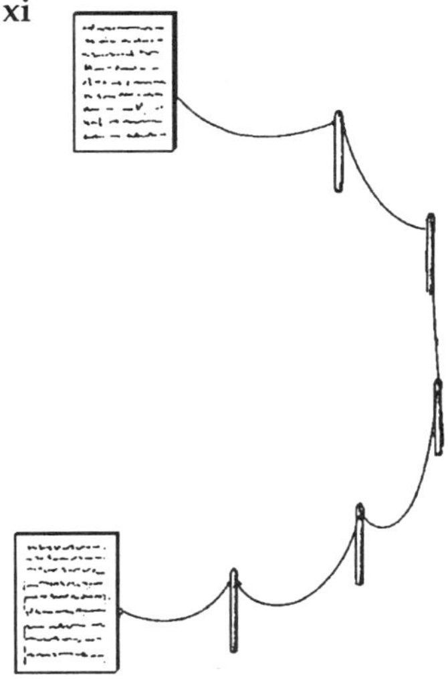

xii. Focusing Machine — This machine helps us understand the importance of focusing as it demonstrates how different individuals focus differently on the same text. It is a three-dimensional representation of the same concept as the canvas for mosaic reading.

xii

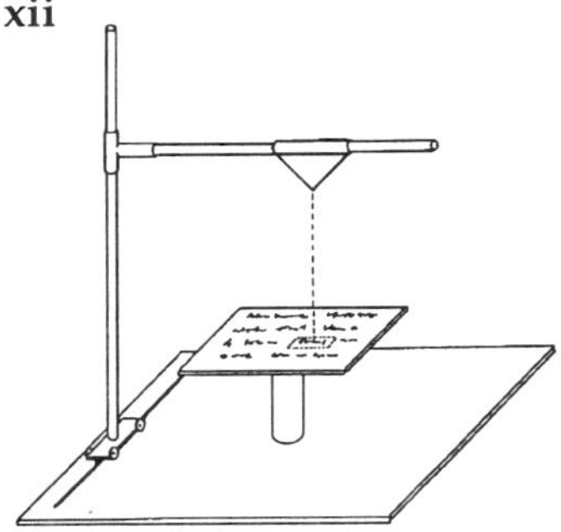

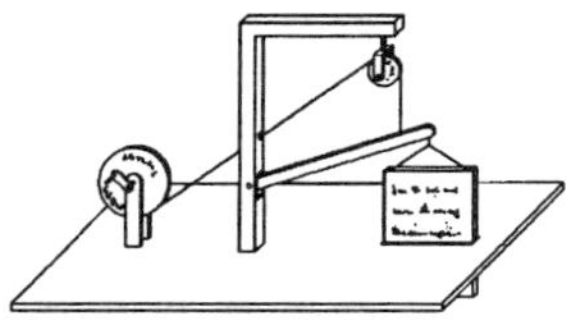

xiii. Machine for Producing Ideas and Turning Them into Text — This complex machine models how one or more evocative words initiate the processes of planning and organizing a text. It is a three-dimensional representation of concepts that have already been explored, as in word-explosion, focusing and linearization.

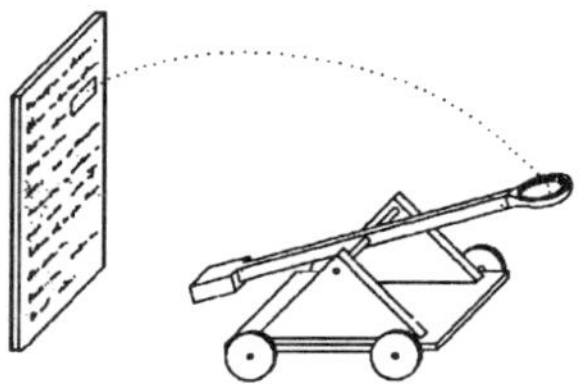

xiv. Textual Catapult — This machine enables us to identify a missing element from the text that can be added, based on the context. The context is the expectation that the text itself creates. This is a three-dimensional representation of a whole set of concepts that have already been explored as in text planning and implicit versus explicit knowledge recognition.

As a result of many transformations that occur at a deep structure level, some global positioning patterns will emerge in texture, which is the potential text that is still to be converted into an actual text.

As a result of transformations and movement at a deep structure level, traces of the communicative positioning will surface and will become visible.

As CPP-TRS is a theoretical model that provides a methodology for recognizing the communicative positioning attitudes and a visual language for making choices visible and accessible, it can be used as a complementary structure in text processing, both in text generation and in the understanding of text .

Surface Structure of a Text

I will now consider what happens at the surface of text.

After deciding texture, the communicative actor must choose and clearly define his final choices. This will not prevent him from changing them again later by taking a consolidated text or text segment and reformulating it globally or locally. I have defined such a process as text-operation and conversion.

Let us now go back to the issue of actualizing text in a way that adequately reflects communicative positioning attitudes that have surfaced as a consequence of deep structure level movements and transformations both on a global level (text) and on a local one (text segments).

What the CPP-TRS framework seeks to describe is the speaker's/hearer's competence of performance, that is the capacity to generate and recognize communicatively positioned texts and text segments. Rephrasing Radford (1988), this is a sort of mental property, that may have two physical manifestations, written or spoken language.

I have addressed the cognitive programme underlying the physical actualization of such performances. Both written and spoken forms of language reflect such cognitive programme based performances. Thus the linguist will not merely study the spoken or written language; he will study language in all its physical dimensions.

I will define the different components which together determine the communicative positioning of texts and text segments. First here are synthetical representations of the deep structure of texture and the surface structure of text respectively (Figures 1.1 and 1.2).

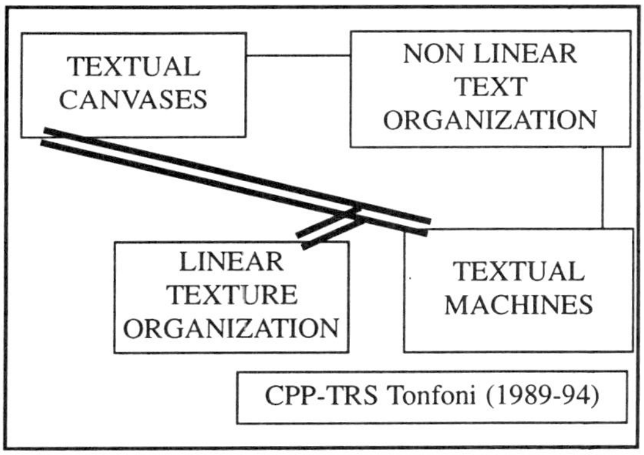

Figure 1.1 — Deep Structure Level of Texture

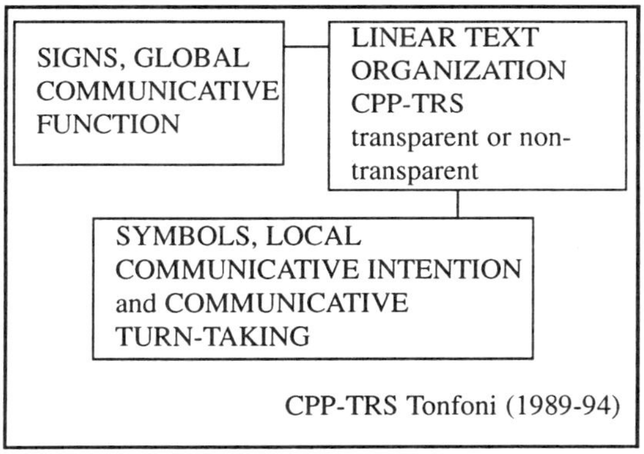

Figure 1.2 — Surface Structure of Text

Let us now analyze the different components that carry specific cues for representing communicative positioning attitudes in the actualized text or text segment.

Signs are global control icons that indicate the communicative function and types of text.

Symbols are local control icons that indicate the communicative intention of text segments.

Turn-taking symbols are local control icons that indicate the role the communicative receiver should play.

Signs and symbols may all be combined to define accurately all the dimensions of positioning.

Signs and symbols are immediate and non-ambiguous; they can be combined and thereby constitute a visual system for communicative positioning attitudes representation.

– *Textual Signs*

Textual signs indicate that a text or text segments must be interpreted as linked, with a specific global communicative function controlling it.

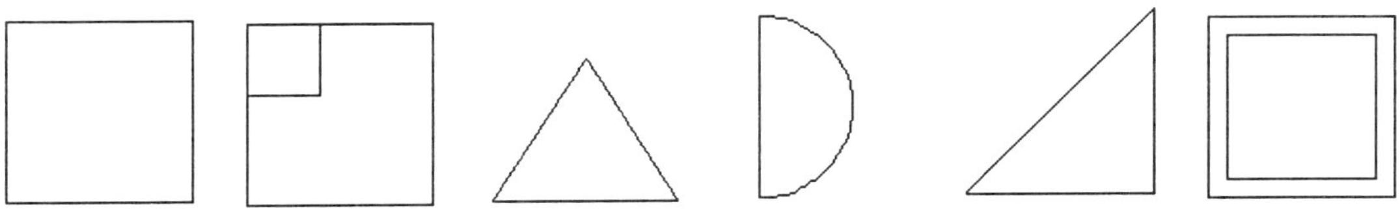

a. Square — *For general information and general story.*

b. Square within a square — *For summary and reduced information taken from a previously provided general information or story.*

c. Triangle — *For a memory text and subjective experience triggered by previously provided general information or story.*

d. Semicircle — *For a particular concept extracted from previously provided general information or story.*

e. Right triangle — *For comment deriving from previously provided general information or story.*

f. Frame — *For a story analogous to another story.*

*g. **Grouped Semicircles** — For concepts that emerge from previously provided general information or story.*

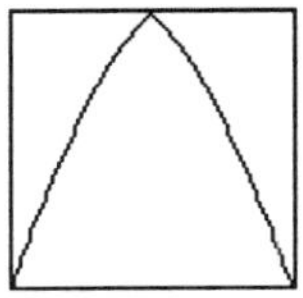

*j. **Inscribed Arcs** — For adding an alternative to a story or previously provided general information.*

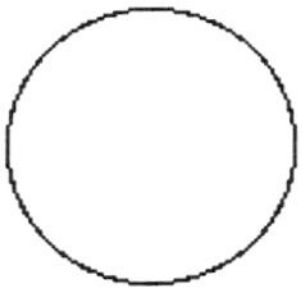

*h. **Circle** — For a global or general concept that emerges from a previously provided general information or story.*

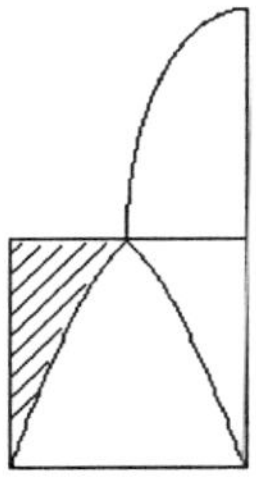

*k. **Opened Text Space** — For opening up a new text segment in a text for an alternative to a story or previously provided general information.*

– *TextualSymbols*

Textual symbols indicate that a text segment is controlled by a specific local communicative intention.

i. Describe — From the Latin "describo", write around. Meaning: the provision of as much information as the author wishes, starting from a point at the middle of the spiral and proceeding by expanding the spiral; there is no need to follow a logical-chronological order; the spiral may be small or large, depending on how much information is being presented.

ii. Define — From the Latin "definio", put limits. Meaning: the provision of only relevant information about a certain point, indicated by the middle point of the square and the limit drawn around it; there is no need to follow any logical-chronological order, but one must select and choose the relevant information to be kept within the square."Define" is "describe" under certain constraints; in a dictionary, the definition of a word or a concept implies that one must choose what is relevant to be written in order to understand the specific meaning.

iii. Narrate — Meaning: the presentation of facts and events by following a logical and chronological order; there are points following each other on a line. The longer the story is, the more points you may add. Arrows indicate the logical reading direction of facts and events. If the story becomes longer, more points are added on the right side and the line becomes longer.

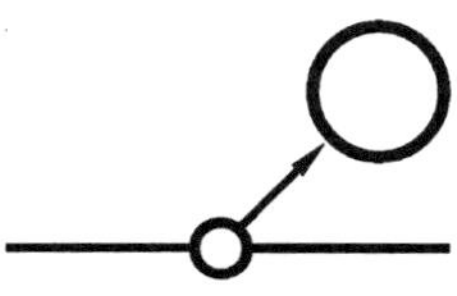

iv. Point out — Meaning: the extraction of a point, specific event or fact, from a narrative (story), focusing on that, adding more information and thereby expanding it. The visual symbol represents the specific point that has been chosen and expanded within a chain of facts and events. Within a story it may represent the need for further information and details about a part of it.

v. Explain — From the Latin "explano" — to unwrap, open up. Meaning: the representation of facts in a cause-and-effect order. It is possible to start from the original cause and descend progressively to a set of effects or move from effects to the original cause. This is why the symbol, a graphic representation of the procedure, works in both directions: from top to bottom and bottom to top.

v

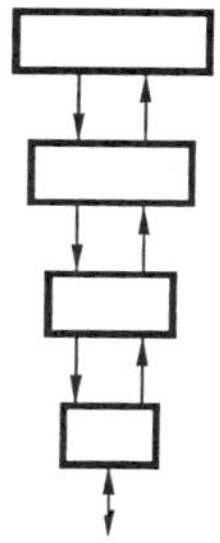

vi

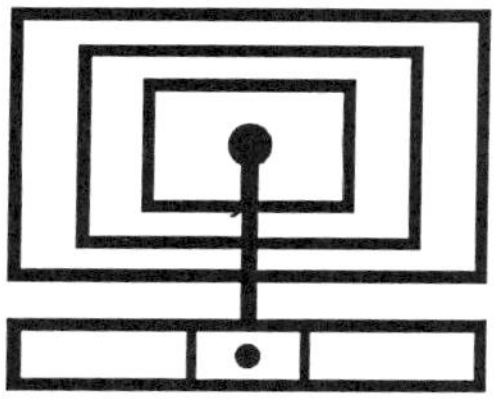

vi. Regress — From the Latin "regredior", go back. Meaning: regression here means giving more information about a certain item within a chain of information. The visual symbol represents the process of focusing on an item and the process of depth information expansion, which is activated just above that point. You may have different levels of regression according to differing information needs.

vii

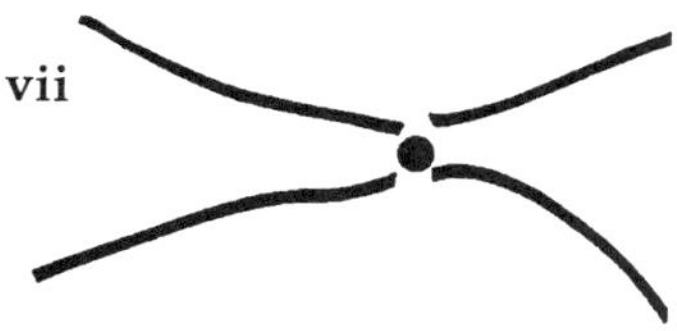

vii. Inform — From the Latin "informo" — put into shape, shape up. Meaning: packaging of information. The visual symbol is double-faced: you can read it from left to right or from right to left. Because of their strong visual impact, symbols (1) and (2) are used to represent the concepts of synthesis and analysis in general and may be added to the other symbols as well (define, describe, explain, etc.).

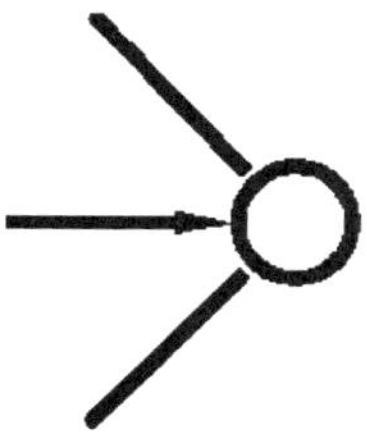

***vii (1). First Phase** —from large to small: synthesis: moving from a large bank of information towards a synthesis (central point).*

***vii (2). Second Phase** — from small to large: analysis: moving from a limited set of data (central point) towards more analytical data.*

viii. Reformulate — From the Latin "reformo reformulo" — change shape and shape again. Meaning: the change of attitude in information packaging: moving from explanation to description or definition or information, etc. In practical terms, this means substituting a cognitive attitude with another, a visual symbol with another. This symbol means "change", "substitute".

xi. Express — From the Latin "exprimo" — push out, press out. Meaning: the provision of personal and emotional opinions about facts. This is the most subjective mode of information packaging and is bound to personal experiences such as "I like / I dislike". The visual symbol represents a visual territory which is open and subject to modification according to personal opinions: an amoeba-like shape.

– *Textual Turn-Taking Symbols*

Textual turn-taking symbols indicate that a text segment will have to be generated or interpreted by specific, local communicative turn-taking.

***a. Major scale** — This symbol indicates that what follows should be interpreted as it is.*

***b. Minor scale** — This symbol indicates a modification to the marked text.*

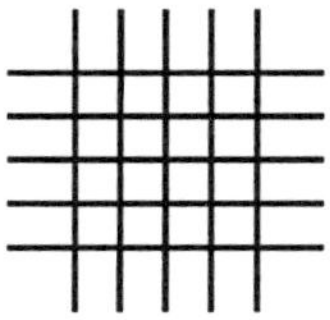

***c. Open or unsaturated rhythm** — This symbol indicates that the text is incomplete. It invites one to add more information if possible.*

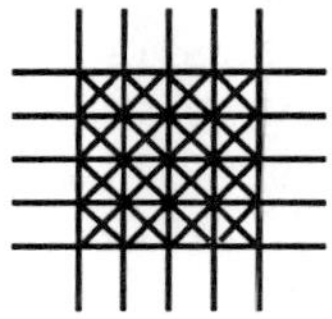

***d. Tight or saturated rhythm** — This symbol indicates that the text is complete.*

The reason why I have defined CPP-TRS as an "unambiguous, fast and effective system for reinforcing natural language" (Tonfoni, 1994) is because it complements natural language with those instructions that represent and are consistent with the "cognitive programme" that everyone has but which are usually hidden and thereby create problems and ambiguity in interpretation. All of these reflect syntactic structures as well and by interpreting them systematically at a different level, many advantages will be found.

Conclusions

Musical notation consists of a set of technically defined terms (andante, allegro, maestoso, etc.) and visual symbols (&) that convey the composer's intention and wishes to those performing or executing a composition. These words and symbols communicate what the notes written on the staff alone cannot.

The communicative actor is like a composer because he/she does not just produce sentences, but produces text with textual instructions that complement the text itself as text execution cues and text interpretation devices. This is how competence of performance can be viewed from a CPP-TRS perspective. Notes are syntactic categories; they form a limited set but may combine in an unlimited number of ways.

This is my contribution to a scientific approach to the study of language and the mind.

A new framework of research will open up for linguists in order to establish the relation between text interpretative devices and the syntactical structures they reflect in different languages, by providing predictable syntactic configurations.

A New Framework for Describing and Explaining Natural Language Processing. A Text Construction Environment

Introduction

Natural language processing needs a comprehensive and powerful metaphor that can be used to reframe complex processes as well as various phenomena in ways that may facilitate both description and explanation.

This is why I have introduced a new metaphor that can identify and name different elements playing different roles in natural language processing.

In order to identify them and see them in action, a Text Construction Environment is an appropriate comprehensive and well defined model representing many actions that take place synchronously and harmoniously.

The models presented are not just representation systems but practical tools acting within a virtual framework.

They are all part of the CPP-TRS Model and part of a consistent and well-defined metaphor representing the complexity of language in action, that is, communication.

A new way of looking at natural language

What is presented here are not just new tools but a completely new framework and way of looking at natural language phenomena. A new scientific paradigm for studying human cognition may both extend knowledge and expand an individual's potential if and only if the individual has adequate interpretative tools with which to talk about cognition, to come to know those cognitive processes that we do not see, but which we know are always active.

In my earlier work (Tonfoni, 1989-94) I defined the concept of cognitive self-reflection as a way to observe, recognize and master cognitive processes by introducing the concept of cognitive self-awareness.

As a process of self-observation, cognitive self-reflection is based on a set of tools that will enable the individual to name qualitatively different actions.

In the Society of the Mind theory (Minsky, 1986) we see an example of what it means to create a strong, comprehensive and well-defined metaphor that describes and explains complex phenomena that would otherwise be invisible and therefore unknown.

The first need for any newly established field of discovery is to name or define the different elements that have been recognized as relevant.

Indeed, no one can refer to elements that have not previously been identified and defined. It is only after having recognized and defined them that it becomes possible to refer to them consistently and to explore their relationships.

Explanation of invisible and therefore unidentified and unknown phenomena has always been necessary. This is what mythology in ancient Greece was meant to be: a description and explanation of undescribed, undefined, and therefore unexplained phenomena. "Myth is a story or belief that attempts to explain a basic truth" (Random House Dictionary, 1978).

By using a metaphor, "a figure of speech in which a term or phrase is applied to something to which it is not literally applicable in order to suggest a resemblance"

(Random House Dictionary, 1978), a scientist can create a virtual world to explain invisible and undefined phenomena.

Virtual reality makes real those things that are unknown and may therefore be consistently and productively applied to those "unnamed phenomena" that become phenomena, "facts, occurrences or circumstances observed or observable" (Random House Dictionary, 1978), only after having been experienced and recognized as such.

The representation of invisible elements or processes is obvious in disciplines such as physics and chemistry: concepts such as "force" and "gravity" in physics use visual representations and mutually shared definitions, while "transformations" or "atoms" in chemistry mean something that could not possibly be experienced directly in other ways.

The impossibility of seeing and sensing such unnamed elements creates the need for highly organized, fully structured and well defined metaphors that can be used in such precise and technical ways that they become the "special technical lexicon of the field".

Unfortunately, this has not happened in all disciplines: in those that look more "real" or "realistic", researchers for quite a long time were misled into thinking that there was no need for models to represent complex and articulated processes.

Let us consider, as an example, linguistics: unfortunately, the existence of real languages and real words and the fact that individuals can actually spell and hear or write and read so-called physically perceptible texts has led researchers to think that the elements to be analyzed are merely there and available like objective data ruled by a consistent control system such as syntax. But this is not accurate: language both in its syntactic articulation and lexical organization is just the surface of a much more articulated and complex set of phenomena.

Chomsky (1957) has demonstrated clearly that sentences as surface syntactic organization structures are merely the end result of a set of processes, which he named "transformations". He concluded that sentences are "generated". A dynamic view of language has been taken further to apply to meaning generation in a wider sense and to "text" (De Beaugrande and Dressler,1981; Ballmer, 1975; Van Dijk, 1969).

These models have all considered language as a device for the organization and representation of knowledge, this being the appropriate target to be addressed.

Knowledge articulation may then be analyzed at different levels, ranging from specifically defined knowledge subdomains to expectations about consistent actions to be taken up, to generalization and abstraction processes that can justify the interpretation process at different levels.

The belief that there is more to text than just words and sentences has also been behind theories such as the Frame theory (Minsky, 1975), the Script theory (Schank, 1977) and, later, the Plan theory (Wilensky, 1983) and the Plot Units theory (Lehnert, 1981).

New interpretative tools

What I propose here is a highly articulated and dynamic metaphor intended to provide interpretation tools that can define and explain invisible aspects of language both in a theoretical framework and as practical tools for supporting communicative actions taking place through language.

Very simply, we can all agree that a word by itself is an element that may trigger a whole range of possibilities in a virtual reality of meaning.

But we can add more: we can create a virtual reality framework for both defining and explaining what is going on in our mind when we talk, write, listen or read, that is, whenever we use language to communicate, that is, to convey text carrying meaning having a specific communicative function as well as various and varying communicative intentions.

This is meant to be a much wider application of a virtual reality framework to language explanation.

One thing is certain: when we talk, write, listen or read, many cognitive processes take place both synchronically and diachronically, which simply means that some of them may take place together and others will take place one at a time or one after the other.

Any model that specifically intends to justify and explain such complex "invisible reality" needs, therefore, to be a virtual reality model based on a consistent and well-defined metaphor, because it must show the different processes taking place in different ways, at different times, at different levels and with different results.

A special metalanguage intended to define, describe and explain linguistic communication, that is communication via language, must be based and grounded within a spatial and dynamic metaphorical reality with different actions taking place as well as different systems for representation. The final result will be the building of an actual text which is the complex, highly articulated, communicative functionalized linguistic entity in process of progressive structuring, termed construction.

A text construction environment needs to be a strong metaphor representing the various cognitive activities that take place, just as different tools are needed to build up a text.

A Virtual Reality Environment for text construction therefore allows the interactive user to be primarily a text builder who experiences text building directly. From now on the User will be called the Chooser as, by assuming such perspective, he/she will interact responsibly with the environment, not merely trying the different possibilities but controlling, directing and acting on the environment itself to ensure the result corresponds to his/her plan.

I hope that the Virtual Reality Community will agree with my decision to redefine the User as the Chooser because this is what Virtual Reality should actually be for: amplifying and giving multiple possibilities, none of which were visible or in existence previously.

'Choosing' means navigating in a wider space of possibilities, interacting with the various scenarios that may occur and then making a decision based on visible criteria.

Controlling a certain process means being able to experience it in its phases by amplifying one's perception of it.

The discovery of a new territory and the exploration of invisible and therefore unknown and unrepresented elements happens many times in science; for example, we have already considered chemical transformations and physical models for knowledge representation.

What we see in such cases is the use of metaphors to represent something that needs to be described, defined and explained, before it can become known and utilized by the research community and a wider audience.

Metaphor, therefore, is quite a productive device for explanation, as in the Society of Mind (Minsky, 1986), which is a dynamic metaphor for describing, defining and explaining what is going on in the mind.

Once a metaphor is understood, it can be used to refer to specific phenomena.

In order to talk about different processes, Minsky (1986) has developed metaphors such as "society", "agency" or coined new names and definitions such as "polinemes", to provide terms to define and describe activities that were invisible.

The "nature" of CPP-TRS

CPP-TRS (Tonfoni, 1989-94) is both a methodology and a language. Through the methodology (CPP) those invisible aspects of communication are identified and represented by the metalanguage (TRS), which complements natural language. Icons in CPP-TRS are not intended to represent words or sentences as a substitute for them; they are rather intended to represent visually what natural language does not convey naturally.

CPP-TRS is a visual language based on a system of 12 canvases, 10 signals, 14 symbols and a set of other dynamic visual schemes. CPP-TRS is based on the fact that every communicative action is the result of a set of cognitive processes, and the whole system is based on the concept that communication may be enhanced by visual planning and organization, therefore raising the visual perception of text. Based on a very simple syntax, CPP-TRS is capable of representing meaning and intention as well as communicating function visually. CPP-TRS is an unambiguous, fast and effective system for reinforcing natural language. It complements natural language by adding certain important elements that are not represented by natural language itself.

In CPP-TRS a certain set of elements, which we do not see because they are not represented by natural language, such as cognitive styles, are identified and named with a verb, with a technical meaning and a corresponding and consistent symbol; communicative types are represented with a name, with a very specific definition and meaning and a corresponding signal.

CPP-TRS is a qualitative model for communication. Once a basic understanding of cognitive styles and communicative types has been reached, the qualitative model of text will turn the quantitative aspect, that is, sentences and paragraphs, into a qualitative representation, in other words, communicative intention and function expectations.

However, symbols and signs are just one aspect of CPP-TRS: there are several other visual dynamic schemes.

Textual machines represent physically and dynamically those cognitive processes that go on in the mind from the most simple to the most complex. They are models that explain things that cannot be seen, a process with different stages that evolve dynamically in time.

The CPP-TRS Model based on canvases, symbols, signs, textual objects and textual machines can be defined as a system that represents visibly that which is invisible in language and that physically models cognitive processes in action.

But CPP-TRS is more than this. By providing the chooser with symbols, signs and machines, it is also a toolkit.

CPP-TRS is therefore both a descriptive, explanatory model dealing with the complexity of text understanding, and an active system for text generation, based on a new way of conceiving text production and text processing.

By understanding the conventional meaning assigned to basic signs — the geometric shapes of squares, triangles, etc. — the chooser will appreciate the meaning of objects that are built up by combining the basic shapes.

To give a very simple example: if a square represents a narrative text, then a cube, which is made of six square elements (faces), is a 3D representation of narrative text, where each

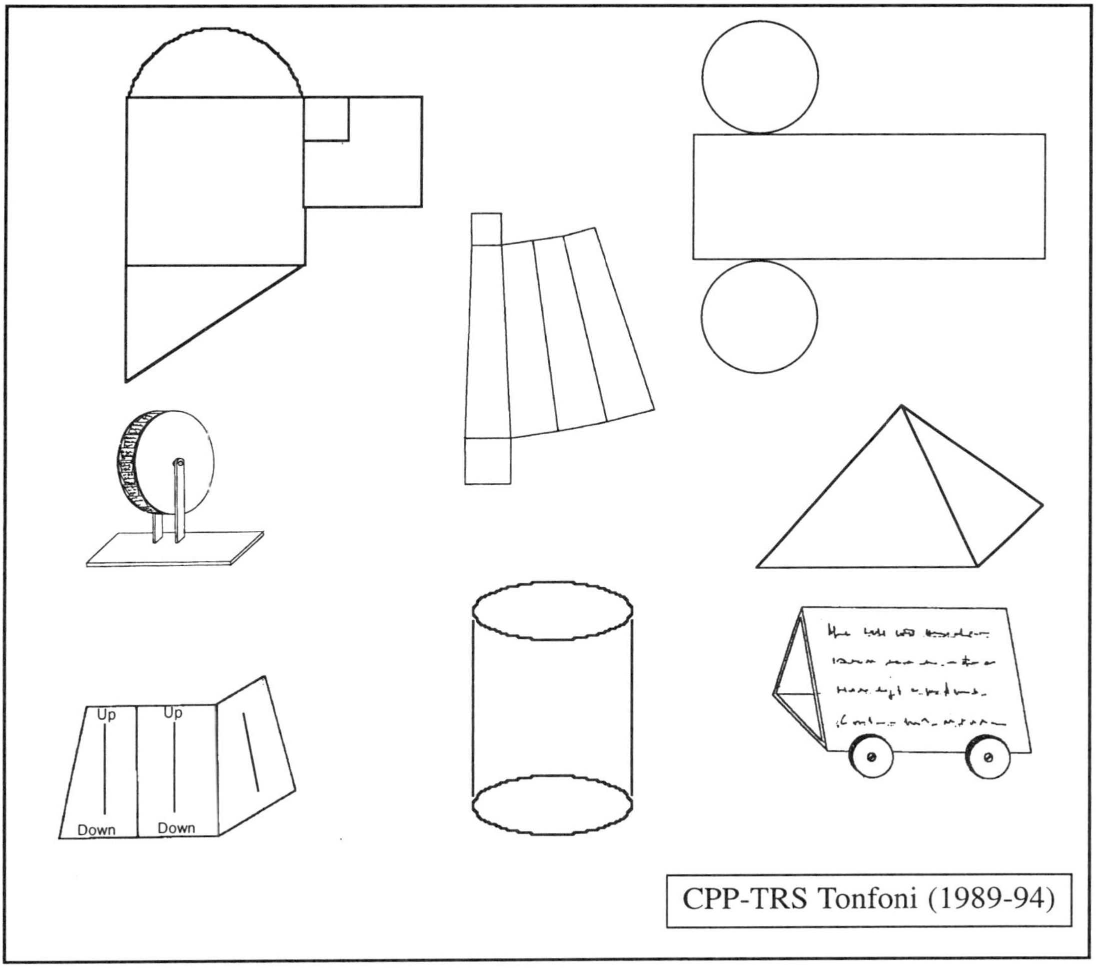

Figure 2.1.

face may be a chapter of a story or a short story in itself. The cube cannot represent another type of text because it would not be consistent, and would be misleading in that it did not respect the agreed semantics.

Textual machines also have this consistency of shape as they are comprised of the same basic shapes that carry specific meanings. The chooser, by learning the basic meanings, can thus learn easily the entire system.

The CPP-TRS model is complex in the sense that it deals with many different aspects of communication, given that communication and language are themselves complex. Complexity does not imply difficulty; rather a model that represents a complex phenomenon needs to be simple. If it is not simple, it does not help to describe, define or explain the fact or set of facts that it is intended to represent. CPP-TRS provides a specific, agreed terminology that uses technical terms in a very precise way, in order to refer and identify the different aspects of a complex process and name them.

A text construction environment

A text construction environment is a virtual environment intended to represent the process of planning and structuring of a text. It is based on a selection of CPP-TRS visual models and metaphors that represent different actions taken in time, both synchronically and diachronically, to produce a constructed "text construction". The term "text construction" is used instead of text production or text generation because by construction we can refer to the material to be processed (information), to the different tools performing different tasks in time (cognitive processes), and to the different shapes and packaging modes the processed material (knowledge) may acquire to become text.

The final result of such operations is the construction of a text. Let us now have a look at Figure 2.1.

The metaphorical construction environment in Figure 1 shows the progressive building up of a text. It is based on CPP-TRS shapes and indicates unambiguously and directly the different communicative functions that the specific text construction will entail. These functions are part of the foundation to ensure that from the planning stage they will remain in the actual building and appear in the final text.

Around the foundation is a set of textual machines that demonstrate the many and various cognitive processes that will take place at different times to turn unprocessed information into sentences, paragraphs and text units, representing processed and packaged knowledge.

Figure 2.1 shows some textual objects that can be added to the text construction to represent other communicative actions, derived from the text according to the specific function each object has been assigned within the CPP-TRS framework.

We saw earlier the textual signs that indicate the various aspects of text development. Textual shapes can be further developed and can evolve into textual objects that show consistency and coherence between the specific shape they have and the kinds of text they contain.

Each textual object carries with it evidence of its particular meaning. Just as the shapes of traffic signs carry specific meanings that are immediately understood, when text is shaped to form a particular textual object, the text shape itself conveys the kind of information needed to interpret text consistently.

In CPP-TRS six textual objects are presented:

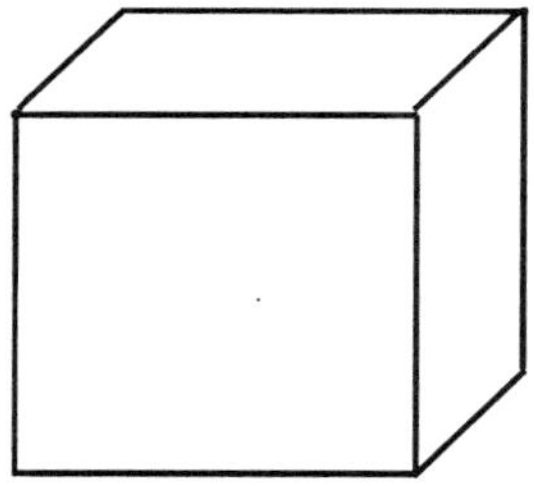

a. Cube — A cube is the individual and collective text-shape and space organization for constructing a story. To construct a story, a text constructor thinks of the text of the story as a cube consisting of six flat, square facets. Each square facet represents a segment of narrative text that tells part of the story. The text constructor begins by constructing the text for each square. To create the story, he folds the six textual squares into a cube. The arrangement of each textual square on the cube demonstrates how the parts of the story relate to one another.

b. Pyramid — A pyramid provides individual and collective text-shape and space organization for a story. A text constructor presents a story that reminds him of other stories, which he adds to the initial one. The same story may remind him of other analogous stories as well, which may then be added too. The pyramid is different from a cube in that it contains personal memories related to a story rather than the story itself.

b

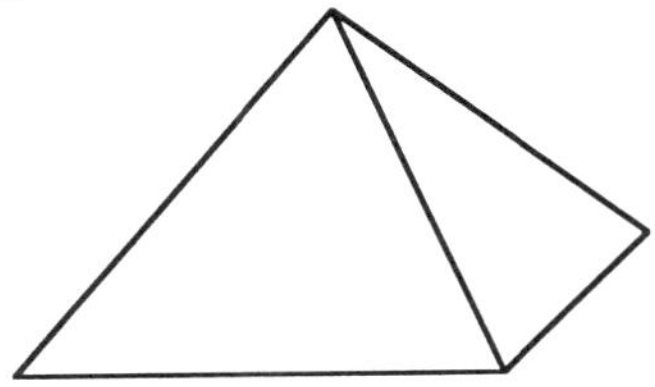

c. Miniature — A miniature provides individual and collective text-shape and space organization for expanding and completing texts. Miniatures were a form of ornamental writing used in the Middle Ages to make the perception of certain texts more pleasant. A miniature textual object has definite parts each containing different kinds of information.

c

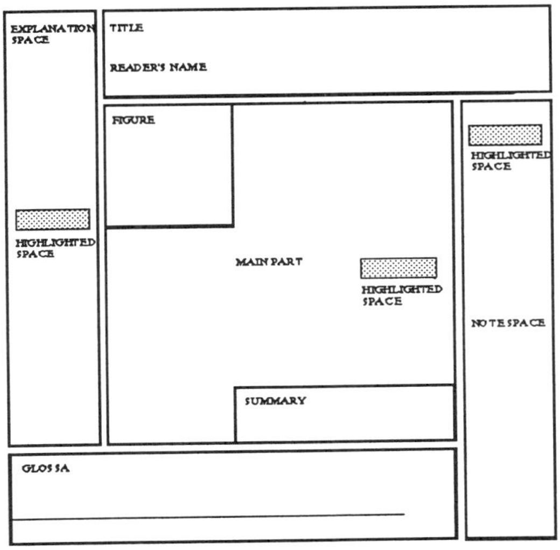

d

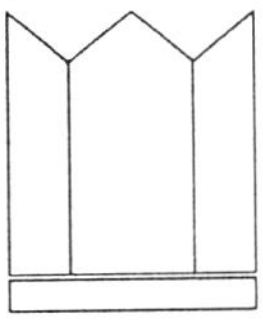

d. Polittico — A polittico is a text-space organization for raising and discussing a topic. Historically, a polittico is a picture made of hinged planes that fold like doors in front of the main scene. In polittico a text constructor raises a topic and asks for comments and opinions.

e

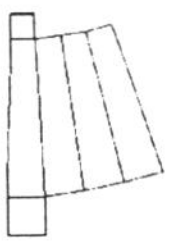

e. Obelisk — An obelisk is a collective text-shape and space organization for recalling a certain story or set of stories well known to a group, and then constructing a common story.

f

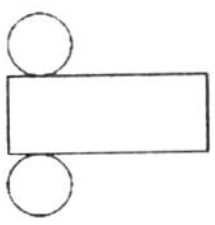

f. Cylinder/Column/Papyrus — A cylinder/column/papyrus is an individual and collective text-shape and space organization for explanatory text construction. A cylinder/column/papyrus is a combination of a cylinder or column and a papyrus, allowing text construction on both the outside and the inside.

Conclusions

The whole metaphor of a text construction environment is a model for the identification and naming of aspects of natural language that cannot be seen and are therefore not usually taken into account. This metaphor provides words that name these aspects and make them obvious. When they are experienced through imagining them in action, they become suitable tools for both self-reflection and further learning.

Text Processing as Text Composition and Text Execution

Introduction

This work provides a new framework for describing and explaining communicative actions involved in text organization and text understanding. Based on a well-defined metaphor required by the complexity of the task itself, the model provides specific visual tools that help us recognize, identify and name those hidden aspects of natural language that are so important to text processing and communicative intercourse.

CPP-TRS (Tonfoni, 1989-94) is both a methodology and a language. Through the methodology (CPP) those invisible aspects of communication are identified and represented by the metalanguage (TRS), which complements natural language. CPP-TRS is a new paradigm where icons or visual schemes are not substitutes for words or sentences, but rather represent visually what natural language does not explicitly convey.

Current trends in text processing were well illustrated in a recent article in AICOM, vol. 7, nrs. 3/4, by S. Geldof, a report on the 1993 Bolzano International School.

Referring to the different approaches that were described, Hovy and Nirenburg (1992) defined "an interlingua as a notation used in Machine Translation systems to represent the propositional and pragmatic meaning of input text" and proposed an organized structure indicating text performance.

On the other hand Kay (1986) underlined the point that bridging the gap between text and interpretation involves "guessing" and that the success of interpretation depends largely on the "ability of the hearer to interpret hints".

Linguists and Artificial Intelligence researchers concerned with natural language processing must always take into account the complexity of natural language. Solutions to problems arising from this may be different but complexity always needs to be dealt with.

Another way to cope with language as a complex system is to define the "context of occurrence". To reduce complexity Kittredge (1992) suggests the concept of natural sublanguage as "a naturally occurring subsystem of language used in reference to a restricted domain".

How CPP-TRS can contribute to managing complexity in natural language

CPP-TRS is a visual language based on a system of 12 canvases, 10 signs and 14 symbols and a wide set of visual dynamic schemes. CPP-TRS is based on the idea that every communicative action is the result of a set of cognitive processes, and the whole system is based on the concept that communication may be enhanced by visually planning and organizing text perception. Based on a very simple syntax, CPP-TRS is capable of visually representing meaning and intention as well as communicative function. CPP-TRS is an unambiguous, fast and effective system for reinforcing natural language. It complements natural language by adding certain important elements that are not represented by natural language itself, such as the communicative function of text and the communicative intention of each paragraph or sentence, as well as the role the text receiver is supposed to play.

Musical notation uses a set of visual symbols to convey the composer's intentions and wishes to those performing or executing a composition. These symbols communicate what the notes written on the staff alone cannot.

The text producer is therefore called a text composer because he or she will not merely produce sentences, paragraphs and text but will also provide the textual instructions that complement text itself as text execution cues.

The text receiver is consequently called a text executor because he or she will not merely receive sentences, paragraphs and text but will also be provided with the visual organization of text instructions for interpreting and understanding the means for executing text.

Text in CPP-TRS is conceived as a musical composition: the text executor "plays" a text, just as a musician executes a composition. To indicate how a text is to be executed, 10 signs and 14 symbols are provided.

In CPP-TRS (Tonfoni 1989-94) the text composer is invited to start from a global perspective of communicative function of the text or the text units and move to the intended meaning of the single paragraph and sentence which is subject to change. The text composer may also ask the text executor to take some specific action by conveying visually his specific request.

As in musical composition, by using CPP-TRS notations a text can be controlled both on a global and local level to facilitate the interpretation process, since CPP-TRS is a consensual system for representing invisible aspects of natural language visually and turning them into specific instructions for text execution.

If text processing can become both text composition and execution, it is evident that the starting point is never merely the sentences or paragraphs but rather the visual organization of the text composition, where sentences and paragraphs are the final result of the process.

According to such a perspective, there is no such process as generic sentence organization where words and sentences flow automatically and unambiguously convey a specific meaning, because this is never true in real communication.

The new approach "from global to local"

Instead of starting with words and stringing sentences together, the text composer will have to decide the communicative function to be attributed to text, the communicative intentions that will vary in the paragraphs and sentences, and the role he will ask the text executor to play.

He will then design the overall communicative structure of the text to go with the text itself. The CPP-TRS-based global and local intention indicators are presented in Figure 3.1. Starting from global control indicators, we first find signs, global control icons that indicate communicative functions within the text. Moving to local control indicators, we find two kinds of symbols.

The first, called cognitive symbols, indicate, paragraph by paragraph or sentence by sentence, communicative intentions that represent specific cognitive processes. Each of these symbols has a technical meaning that relates to a cognitive process and identifies a specific intention to be indicated within the text composition for consistent text execution.

The second kind of symbols, called turn-taking symbols, indicate the kind of interaction the text composer wants to have with the text executor. Turn-taking symbols are meant to

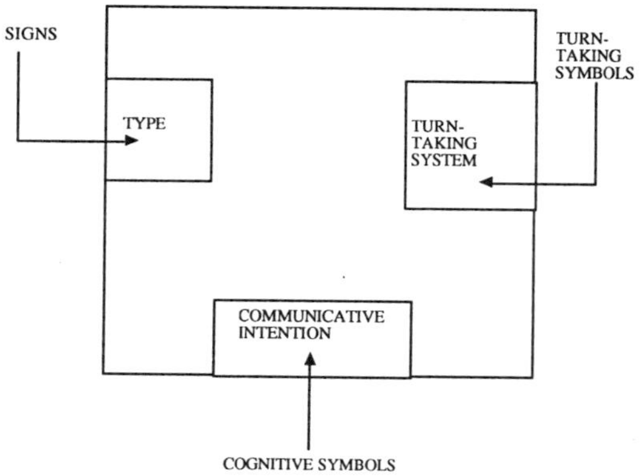

Figure 3.1

indicate when, how and why the text executor should actively become part of the text composition during the text execution process. Turn-taking symbols are the most interactive indicators, allowing the text executor to change, add or remove parts which are in the text composition.

A mental keyboard to compose and play texts

The composing of a text according to CPP-TRS implies a previous organization of text both on a global level (signs) and on a local level (symbols). CPP-TRS may thus be defined in terms of a visual notation system that is as consistent as the system of punctuation.

The system of punctuation is conventional in that it was created *ex novo* and consensual in that everybody agrees to use it in a particular way. It does not change and represents pauses and intonation in language. The punctuation system complements natural written language and adds to it what is there in oral language but would otherwise be missing in written texts.

The CPP-TRS visual system is no different to the punctuation system in that it represents

Figure 3.2

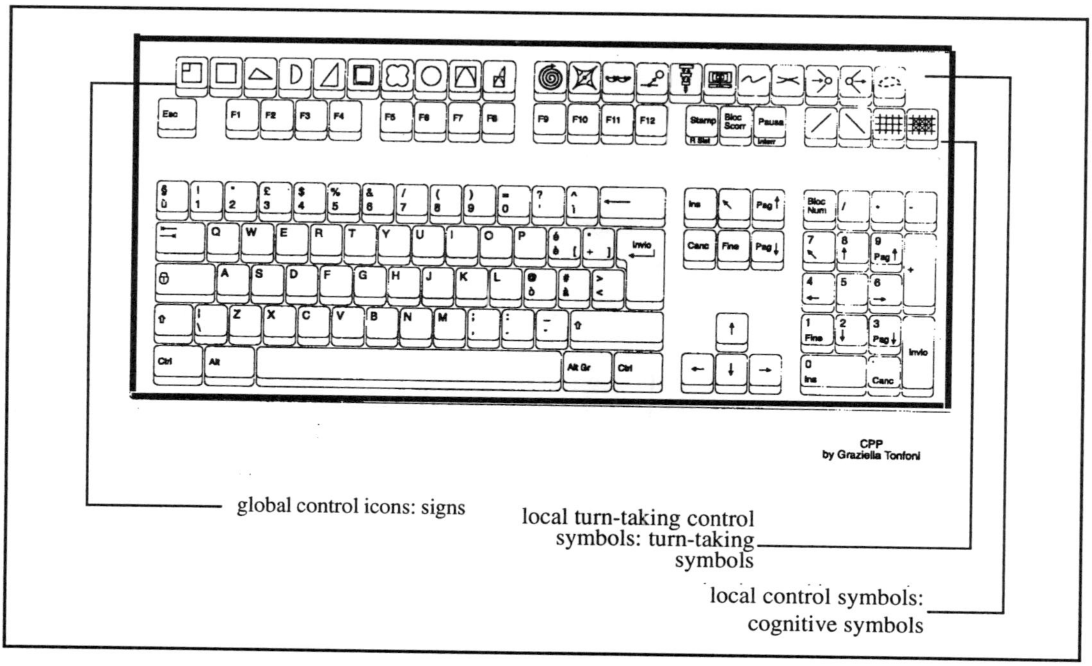

visually those elements, such as communicative intention, communicative function and communicative turn-taking, that are invisible but important to the understanding of a text in the way the text composer intends. CPP-TRS is both a conventional and natural metalanguage that makes explicit from the beginning what otherwise is left to arbitrary interpretation. Making text more explicit by adding visual conventions enhances the final understanding by providing the appropriate "hints of guessing" (Kay, 1986).

Let us now look at Figure 3.2, which shows the CPP-TRS-based keyboard.

In a CPP-TRS (Tonfoni, 1989-94) perspective the traditional process of creating a message is reversed. Instead of starting with words and sentences, the text composer must first understand his own intention, then design the structure of the text, and finally select sentences and words for it. This approach avoids the limitations of the traditional approach by making communicative intentions explicit at the very beginning.

– *A mental scanner to segment, mark off and execute texts*

The executing of a text by interpreting CPP-TRS notations allows text segments that must be played according to specific instructions to be identified.

Just as a scanner is able to reproduce and reprint a certain text, a mental scanner metaphor helps natural language processing experts to programme the text for a certain operation that can either replicate or modify the original text structure, either locally or globally. By keeping CPP-TRS notations transparent, it will always be possible to trace back the kind of operation performed on the structure of the text.

The CPP-TRS based scanner is shown in Figure 3.3. The transparent use of CPP-TRS allows the text executor to read signs and symbols both with the text and as a visual language on its own that carries information about text that would otherwise be implicit and not linguistically conveyed.

What do CPP-TRS icons actually mean?

describe

define

We can agree that there is no need constantly to explain the difference between a comma (,) and a full stop (.). We know the difference because we can hear the pauses in speech and compare them: one is shorter and the other longer.

CPP-TRS works the same way. The text composer will have to pay specific attention to what he and others do with language in order to recognize the difference between *describe* and *define*.

The punctuation system is a consensual system for representing visually pauses and intonation that would otherwise be missing from written language. CPP-TRS is a consensual system for visually representing communicative functions, communicative intentions and communicative turn-taking.

In text composition, a significant increase in the level of understanding is achieved by sending visually and unambiguously communicative hints to trigger "intended guessing".

In text execution, by following CPP-TRS instructions the text may also be reshaped so that it can be filed and retrieved carrying the intended interpretation visually. CPP-TRS can be defined as a "metalanguage". In mastering CPP-TRS anyone should be able to use it as naturally as they do the punctuation system without putting constraints and restrictions on possible uses.

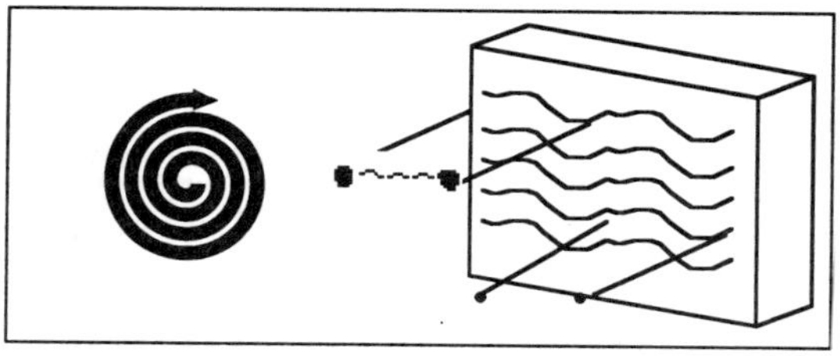

Figure 3.3 - Stage A — Local Scanning for communicative intentions by identifying segments and marked-off portions of text.

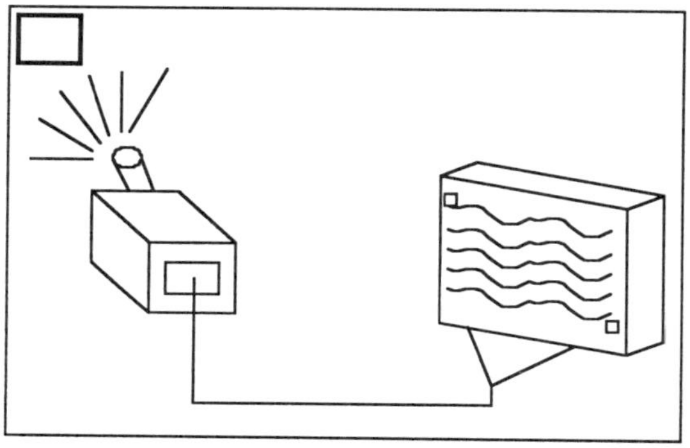

Figure 3.3 - Stage B — Global Scanning for searching and identifying communicative functions of the text or text unit.

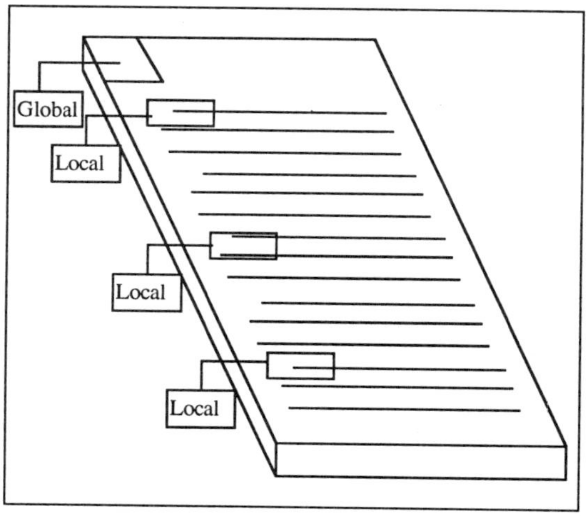

Figure 3.3 - Stage C — Globally and Locally Scanned text or text unit ready to be executed or reformulated either globally or locally according to turn-taking instructions.

CPP-TRS is easily acquired after some training because it is merely the visual representation of what happens to anyone who composes or executes a text, that is uses natural language to communicate.

– What kind of instructions do signs in CPP-TRS provide?

Signs are global control icons intended to convey the global communicative function of a text or text unit. They are consensually shared both by the text composer and the text executor. Let us now analyze them:

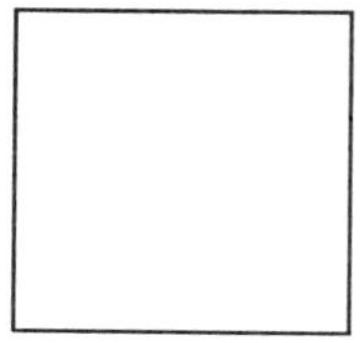

Square — This sign is used by the text composer to indicate that the text is either a story or general information. The sign therefore indicates to the text executor that the text needs to be executed as either a story or general information.

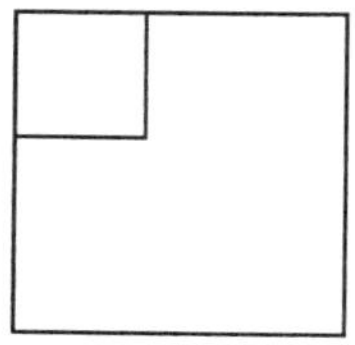

Square within a square — This sign is used by the text composer to indicate that the text is either summarized or reduced from a more extended text. The sign indicates to the text executor that the text needs to be summarized or reduced.

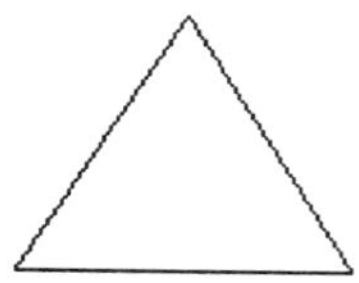

Triangle — This sign is used by the text composer to indicate that the text is about memories or personal events. The sign indicates to the text executor that the text needs to be executed as such and not, for instance, as an objectively informative text.

Semicircle — This sign is used by the text composer to indicate that a specific concept or abstraction has been taken out of a more extended text.

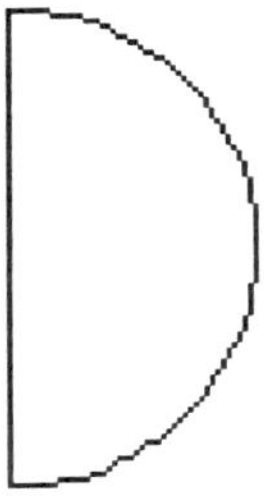

The sign indicates to the text executor that the word or concept presented must be abstracted from an extended text.

Right Triangle — This sign is used by the text composer to indicate that the text is a comment to a story or general information. The sign indicates to the text executor that the text must be executed as a comment to another text and not as an isolated communicative event.

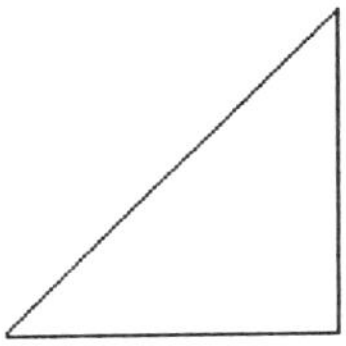

Frame — This sign is used by the text composer to indicate that the text is analogous and refers back to another text. The sign indicates to the text executor that the text needs to be linked up to another one.

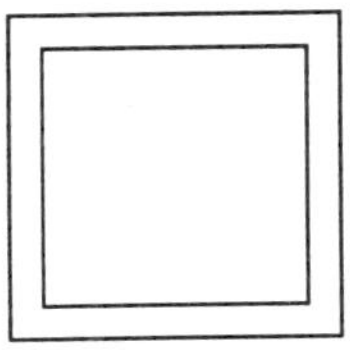

Grouped Semicircles — This sign is used by the text composer to indicate that more concepts (here 3) have been abstracted out of a text. This sign indicates to the text executor that the words or concepts presented must be executed as the result of a set of abstraction processes.

Circle — This sign is used by the text composer to indicate that one word or global concept has been abstracted to represent the text. The sign indicates to the text executor that the one word or global concept presented must be executed as the result of an overall abstraction process.

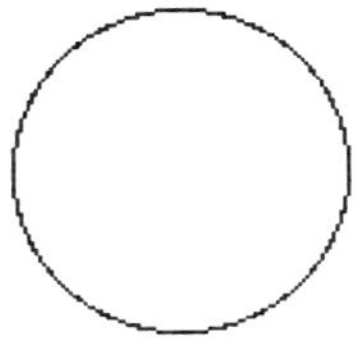

Inscribed Arcs — This sign is used by the text composer to indicate that an alternative development of a story, or additional information, will be provided.

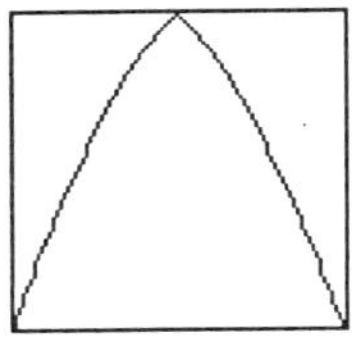

The sign indicates to the text executor that the text is unfinished and awaits some alternative event or information.

Opened Text Space — This sign is linked to the one above (inscribed arcs); it is used by the text composer to indicate alternative information. This sign, together with the one above, indicates to the text executor that the text presented must be executed with the alternative information.

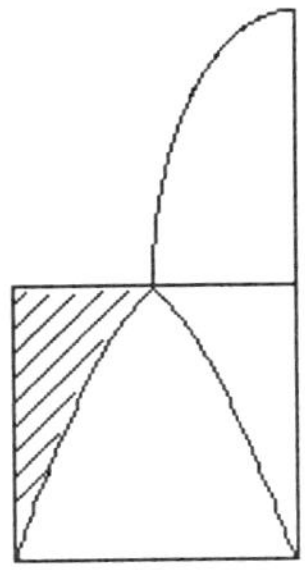

By recognizing the message unambiguously and consensually conveyed by the sign, text execution is facilitated.

Being global control icons representing the communicative function of a text or text unit, signs play the same role different keys play in a musical score, attributing to notes the corresponding values. Signs attribute to a text consistent communicative values.

– *What kind of instructions do cognitive symbols give in CPP-TRS?*

Cognitive symbols are local control icons intended to convey specific communicative intentions, paragraph by paragraph or sentence by sentence. They are consensually shared both by the text composer and by the text executor.

If signs have been designed to be consensually agreed upon and shared, cognitive symbols also visually represent the kind of instructions they give and are therefore self-explanatory.

Let us now analyze ten cognitive symbols that represent specifically defined cognitive processes:

Describe, from the Latin "describo", write around. This symbol is used by the text composer to indicate that a certain paragraph or sentence is composed in a descriptive style and therefore conveys a descriptive intention. It indicates that as much information as wished is provided; there is no need to follow a logical-chronological order, depending on how much information is being presented. Visually, the spiral may be small or large, proceeding from the middle point by expanding it.

Define, from the Latin "definio", put limits. This symbol is used by the text composer to indicate that a certain paragraph or sentence is used as a definition. Only the relevant information about a certain word or concept is provided. There is a need to select only relevant information in order to understand the specific meaning. This is what happens in a dictionary. Visually, the middle point of the square is constrained by the square itself, which indicates a limited meaning.

Narrate, from the Latin "narro", tell a story. This symbol is used by the text composer to indicate that a certain paragraph or sentence is a narrative and conveys a narrative intention. Facts and events are presented by following a logical and chronological order. Visually, arrows indicate the logical reading directions of facts and events. If the story becomes longer, more points may be added on the right and the line becomes longer.

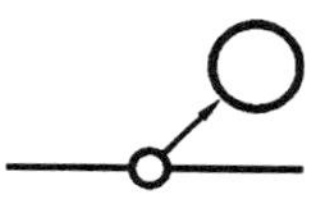

Point out means highlighting a specific event or fact from a narrative text and focusing on it by adding more information, thereby expanding it. This symbol is used by the text composer to indicate that something is being pointed out or highlighted.

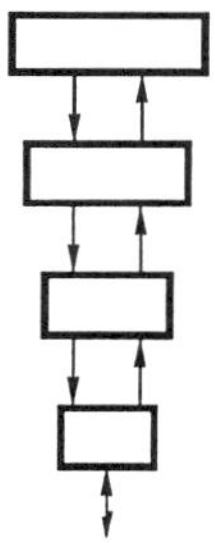

Explain, from the Latin "explano", unwrap, open up. This symbol is used by the text composer to indicate that a certain paragraph or sentence is an explanation. Facts are given in a cause and effect order, that is, linked in a logical chain. Visually, the graph works from top to bottom and from bottom to top since an explanation may start from the original cause and work back progressively to a set of effects, or it may proceed from the effects and go back to the original cause.

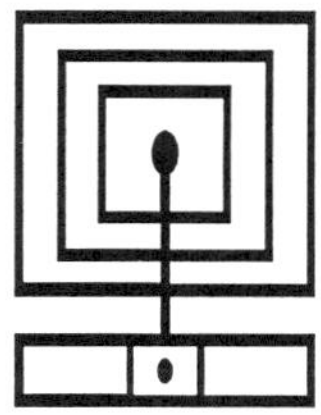

Regress, from the Latin "regredior", go back. This symbol is used by the text composer to indicate that a certain paragraph or sentence is regressive. More information is given about a certain item within a chain of information.

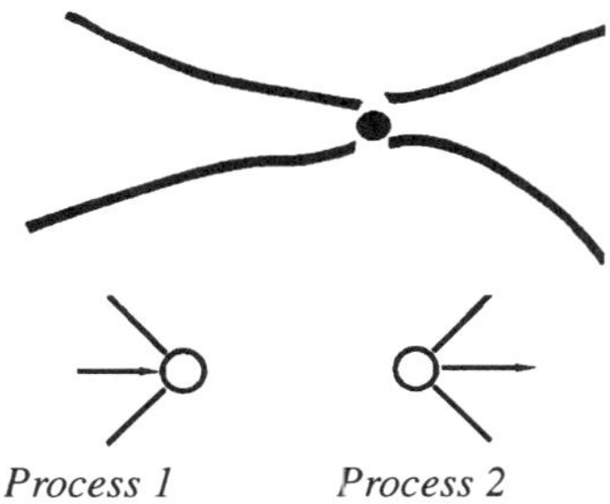

Inform, from the Latin "informo", put into shape, shape up. This symbol is used by the text composer to indicate that a certain paragraph or sentence is meant to be informative. On a general level, it means that information is organized and on a more specific level it indicates two different processes: first, moving from a large database towards a synthesis, and second, moving from a limited set of data towards a more analytical data search. Visually, the symbol is double faced: it can be read left to right, representing both Process 1 — from large into small (the central point) — synthesis, and Process 2 — from small (the central point) into large — analysis. Because of their strong visual impact both symbols are used to represent the concepts of synthesis and analysis and may be added to and combined with other symbols as well.

Express. from the Latin "exprimo" – push out, press out. Personal and emotional opinions about facts are provided. This is the most subjective mode of information packaging and bound to personal experiences such as "I like / I dislike". The visual symbol represents a visual territory which is open and subject to modification according to personal opinions; it is amoeba shaped.

Reformulate, from the Latin "reformo, reformulo", to change shape and reshape. This symbol is used by the text composer to indicate that a certain paragraph or sentence is undergoing a major change of style in text composition and that the text executor will have to watch out for a major exchange. Attitude to information organization must be changed such as moving from explanation to description, basically substituting one cognitive style and intention with another. Visually, the change and substitute instruction is represented as a shift. The symbol may be made more specific by showing explicitly the style and communicative intention from which one is moving to the end style and communicative intention by using the corresponding symbols.

Since local control icons for representing styles and communicative intentions change frequently in the course of the text, cognitive symbols play the same role that "adagio/andante/maestoso" notations play in music by being indicators of what is intended.

– *What kind of instructions do turn-taking symbols give in CPP-TRS?*

Turn-taking symbols are local control icons that convey specific instructions about the kind of role the text executor needs to play when requested by the text composer. Let us now analyze the four cognitive symbols representing pairs of opposing instructions:

This symbol is used by the text composer to indicate to the text executor that the paragraph or sentence or marked off portion of text must be executed exactly the way it has been composed. Here the text composer plays the major role by indicating how to execute text using a consistent set of signs and symbols. The symbol is called major scale.

This symbol is used by the text composer to indicate that the paragraph or sentence or marked off portion of text is meant to be modified before being executed. Assigning the text executor this important role, the text composer steps back for a while and plays a minor role. He takes turn with the text executor, who is now himself the text composer. The original text composer now plays a minor role. The symbol is called minor scale.

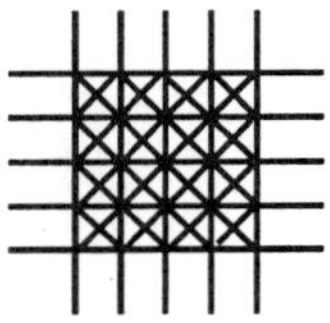

This symbol is used by the text composer to indicate that the paragraph or sentence or marked off portion of text is meant to be executed without any additions. It is complete, possibly a bit too rich: in any case it contains all the information the text composer considers to be relevant. The symbol is called a tight or saturated rhythm.

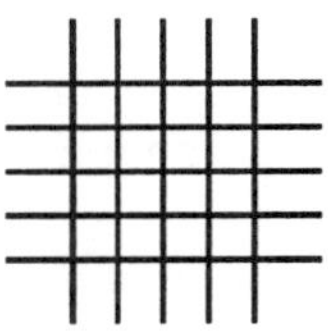

This symbol is used by the text composer to indicate that the paragraph or sentence or marked off portion of text is incomplete. It needs to be completed with additional information, which the text composer may not have or may not be willing to give. He therefore explicitly asks the text executor to become part of the composition process by adding information himself. The symbol is called an open or unsaturated rhythm.

As a local control icon for regulating turn-taking in the course of text composition and execution, turn-taking symbols play an extremely important role in regulating the level of interactivity between the text composer and the text executor.

As with music, the execution of a certain text may underline the role of text executor by making visible the interpretation of text, just as Beethoven's music may be executed differently by Abbado or Muti or Furtwängler. It is hard to say why and how those versions are so different yet still respect the instructions given by Beethoven. A musician can see what these differences are by referring to a specific music metalanguage; the listener may just feel them, without necessarily being able to define them.

The same things can be seen in natural language processing. CPP-TRS is a metalanguage which is intended to allow natural language experts to experience and name, and therefore identify, the different composition and execution possibilities of a text.

There has always been awareness of the complexity of language and interpretation of the existing gaps: CPP-TRS is a consensual metalanguage that can be used to refer consistently to text processing activities in a way that can be consensually shared.

If natural language experts have to define every time what they are doing about language, if there are no consensually agreed categories to refer to, redundancy, ambiguity and fuzziness will create a real barrier to a scientifically based model of description.

The building up of the CPP-TRS Model (Tonfoni, 1989-94) has taken the author many years of checking the cognitive validity of the selected categories and testing their value in actual text processing as well in interlingual and intercultural understanding.

The model has been kept rather simple: if it had been more complex it would have added problems instead of solving them.

The model is therefore simple but well developed enough that it can represent the complexity of natural language: what may not be fully explained by one symbol or sign may be explained by a combination of them.

Both signs and symbols have been chosen and designed not only to match sentences and paragraphs and text units as interpretation devices, but also because they can be combined to raise the overall semantics of the text and can be substituted one with another.

They can be used frequently or infrequently. What matters is not how often they are used but how well they convey the choices of the text composer and text executor.

CPP-TRS can also be defined as a textual prosody. Cruttenden (1986) states that prosodic features may extend over varying domains, either short or long stretches. In the same way, CPP-TRS prosodic features may apply to text segments of various lengths. Of course, the distinction is not always clear-cut; nevertheless the notation system will help to avoid any ambiguity by allowing a combination of signs and symbols to be used synchronously if needed.

CPP-TRS is not just a new metaphor for modelling text; it is also a toolkit for text composition and execution

In order to provide natural language research with both a new terminology and new metaphors to indicate elements and aspects of language that are otherwise vague, subject to personal interpretation or merely undefined, new definitions of specific cognitive processes and new icons for representing invisible aspects of language have been introduced, described and explained.

CPP-TRS is a unifying framework that allows research in natural language processing to take different directions, to be supported by a commonly shared terminology while still retaining its originality and diversity of perspectives.

The variety of approaches that characterize natural language processing research may be considered a sign of a positive attitude towards the many ways of managing the complexity inherent in natural language. A common framework may help better to identify common problems and different ways to approach them.

CPP-TRS may also be defined as a set of practical tools. The system may thus be used for very practical purposes in various domains.

The mental keyboard, presented above, is a metaphor for rethinking the text composition process, but it may also be turned into a prototype keyboard, with CPP-TRS signs and symbols available for transparent use in text processing as an extension of the punctuation system and word processing facilities.

The same is true for the mental scanner, which is on the one hand a metaphor for rethinking text execution through a physical and defined model, but may also be considered a model of an actual scanner, where CPP-TRS signs and symbols are made available for filtering, filing and revising processed texts.

Conclusions

A metaphor that represents a global framework for modelling a well-defined and complex research domain, such as natural language processing, may become a whole set of tools.

This is what the CPP-TRS Model and Metalanguage are intended to do.

On Visual Text Planning, Processing and Programming

Introduction

Relevant research is taking place in the field of the integration of natural language and vision processes. Significant analogies can be found between visual perception and language perception, as pointed out by Winston (1992). The weakness of interactions between image processing and natural language processing was found by Marr (1982), Ballard and Brown (1982) and Joshi (1991). A common semantics of language and vision has been thoroughly analyzed by Ó Nualláin and Smith (1994). An important exploration in the field is by McKevitt (1994a, 1994b).

An interesting survey on literature of computational models for integrating linguistic and visual information is by Srihari (1994). Research on iconic languages by Mealing and Yazdani (1990) has shown the need for accurate research in icon production.

Research into the integration of natural language and vision has grown very large, as we can see in McKevitt (1994c, 1994d).

CPP-TRS by Tonfoni (1989-94) can be defined as a computational model for integrating qualitative reasoning about natural language texts and visual representation of the newly defined qualitative communication categories.

Visual Text Planning

The basic metaphors used in CPP-TRS are taken from drawing and painting. The first metaphor is the canvas. For a visual artist, a canvas is a basic support for his work and is the first consideration for his execution of the work. A canvas can be fine and smooth or coarse and rough, depending on the tightness or looseness of its weave. A visual artist chooses a canvas partly because of the particular characteristics of its texture. A finely textured canvas is appropriate for detailed, precisely drawn or painted work, while a coarse canvas may be worked for a thick, bold application of paint. Thus texture in CPP-TRS (Tonfoni, 1989-94) has a radically different meaning from that found in current literature.

Coherence of the text is investigated in terms of texture, a lexico-grammatical pattern that signals the relationship between individual messages and is identified in terms of cohesive ties and cohesive devices (Halliday and Hasan, 1985). Coherence is therefore investigated with respect to register in terms of text-structure as related to a Generic Structure Potential (GSP) associated to text (Halliday and Hasan, 1985). Coherence as text structure is determined by semantic relations that describe how sentences and text units are linked together to form and continue discourse (Hobbs, 1979; and Mann and Thompson, 1987).

Texture in CPP-TRS is a set of unprocessed sentences and text paragraphs ready to be planned and organized according to the communicative intention of the text planner.

Just as a visual artist chooses a canvas with an appropriate texture, a text planner needs to decide which kind of "texture" his text will have. The texture of text has to do with the density of information conveyed (quantitative level). Depending on the particular communicative purpose of the text, what the text planner intends to achieve and what the text is actually for (qualitative aspect), the texture of the text may be more or less dense.

This means that the qualitative aspect of language will regulate and control the quantitative level.

Not only does the metaphor of canvas carry the property of texture, it also provides a visual context for the process of text planning. After planning a canvas with the right texture, that is a consistent quantity of information, the planner establishes perspective, point of view and focus, and possibly a cliché for the drawing or painting. The perspective identifies how the text planner positions himself/herself; the point of view shows what the text planner selects as most relevant; the focus indicates what is topical; and the cliché displays how the text planner deals with organizing a communicative space in which the reader may move around.

From a CPP-TRS perspective, the reader is the visual text processor. A visual text processor is an active individual who interprets the visual text planner's communicative intention, as well as the communicative function of the text, that is the qualitative level of communication within the text itself as articulated in sentences, paragraphs and text units, representing the quantitative aspect of information.

According to CPP-TRS (Tonfoni, 1989-94) text processing may be enhanced by bringing to light those aspects of meaning that are invisible, that are not conveyed linguistically within the text but are relevant for text interpretation.

To cope with this problem, both global and local planning of text is conceived visually. Only after texture is organized visually may the text planner use sentences and paragraphs.

The CPP-TRS approach is consistent with the Society of Mind Theory (Minsky, 1986), which contends that many specific cognitive processes take place before actual language, sentences and texts are formulated.

The difficulties in text processing are therefore explored and addressed before text occurs, in the cognitive planning of it. The difficulties we encounter in organizing a text are usually the result of cognitive, not linguistic, problems.

In CPP-TRS the text planner is asked to start from a global perspective on the communicative function of the text he/she is going to organize and to move towards a local consideration of the communicative intention of each text unit, paragraph and sentence. He/she must also define the role he/she wants the text processor to play.

CPP-TRS provides a set of canvases that are visual schemes and global and dynamic representations of communicative actions that may be taken in the course of text planning. Canvases are thus visual dynamic schemes that represent the various communicative actions that may be taken and are therefore self-reflective tools. Once the text planner has an overall global view of his/her textual plan by visually representing it, he/she may then proceed to the detailed organization and structuring of the text itself.

Before organizing the text, text must be conceived as an open possibility, which can be further planned and organized from a multitude of perspectives and points of view, with many different focuses, intentions and organizational considerations.

Canvases visually represent possible actions that could be taken to plan text and retain the visual planning of the linguistic part, that will emerge in the final result.

Let us now look at the CPP-TRS model which both identifies and names the different processes and actions that take place when a text is structured. It provides the text planner and the text processor with new visual tools that can make visible what is invisible within the text itself.

By enhancing Visual Text Perception, both text planner and text processor share visual semantics about the qualitative level of the text. The CPP-TRS approach therefore differs radically from traditional approaches to organizing text, which assume that individuals create meaning and intentions after having connected words and sentences. In fact, planning of meaning and intention comes first, with words and sentences coming last, as we can see in Figure 4.1.

Canvases are visual dynamic representations of actions, which need to be used in text planning on a very general level.

From canvas, the text planner goes directly to linear text organization, keeping the visual schemes together with the text itself. He/she can then be defined as a Visual Text Planner because he/she is explicitly declaring the communicative plan he/she has chosen by making it obvious and keeping it with the text.

As a result, the text processor will be able to interpret the text more easily by knowing the communicative plan and by being directly assisted in the interpretation process by being told the kind of communicative action that has been taken. The visual processor will therefore receive both quantitative information (sentences, paragraphs, text units) and qualitative information (the kind of communicative action taken to produce the text).

In CPP-TRS (Tonfoni, 1989-94), by proceeding from canvas into linear text organization the visual text planner keeps the overall general plan of the text and the kind of action taken (Figure 4.1, Line A). By "taking" Line A the visual text processor receives a general

Figure 4.1

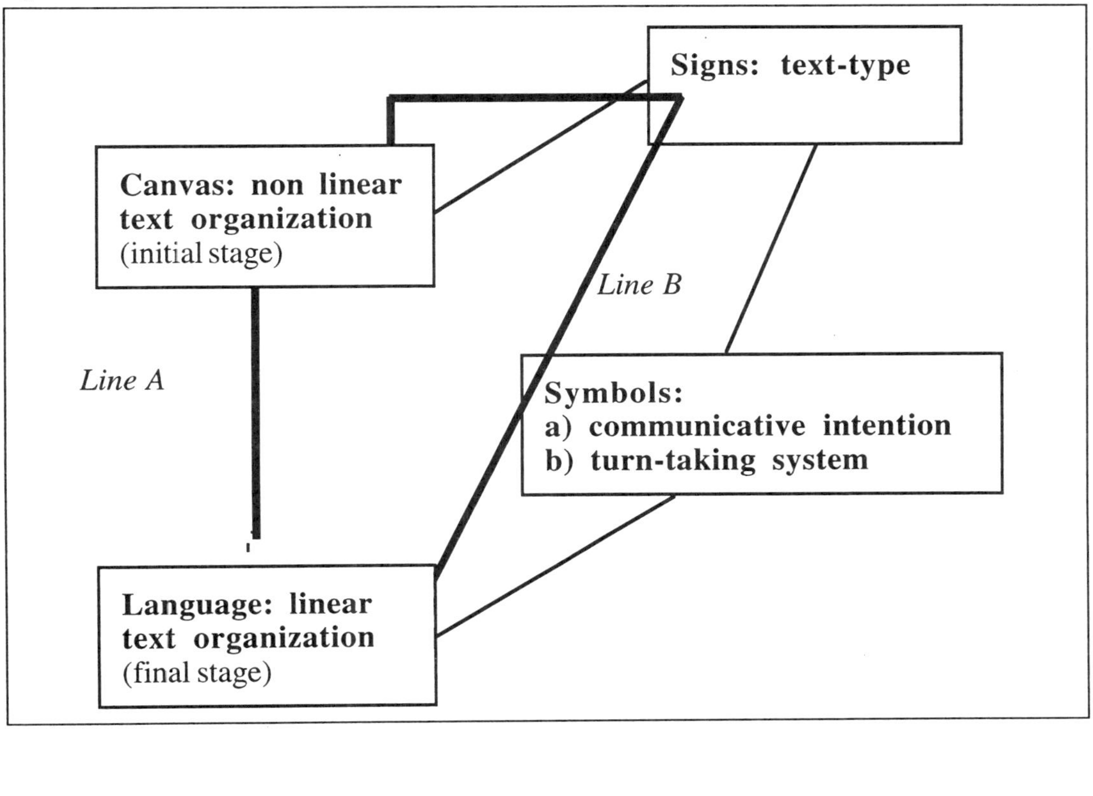

level of qualitative information, which is much more than what he would receive from a traditionally processed text without the qualitative information.

But the visual text planner may wish even more qualitative information to be added to the text and to be available to the visual text processor by accessing other visual tools provided by CPP-TRS.

Let us now follow Line B in Figure. 4.1: Once the visual text planner has given a general view of the kind of action taken on text, he/she can then move towards the more detailed planning of different paragraphs and sentences both on a global and a local level. CPP-TRS starts from a global perspective of communicative functions, and moves towards the role the text processor should play, as shown in Figure 4.2.

Signs are global control icons for explaining the communicative type and function of a text unit.

Symbols are local control icons for explaining the communicative intention and style of sentences or paragraphs.

Turn-taking symbols are local control icons for explaining the role the visual text processor should play, either in adding more information to the text or in processing it the way it is.

The level of qualitative information about the text may vary according to either the visual text planner or visual text processor and is mutually agreed upon.

Figure 4.2

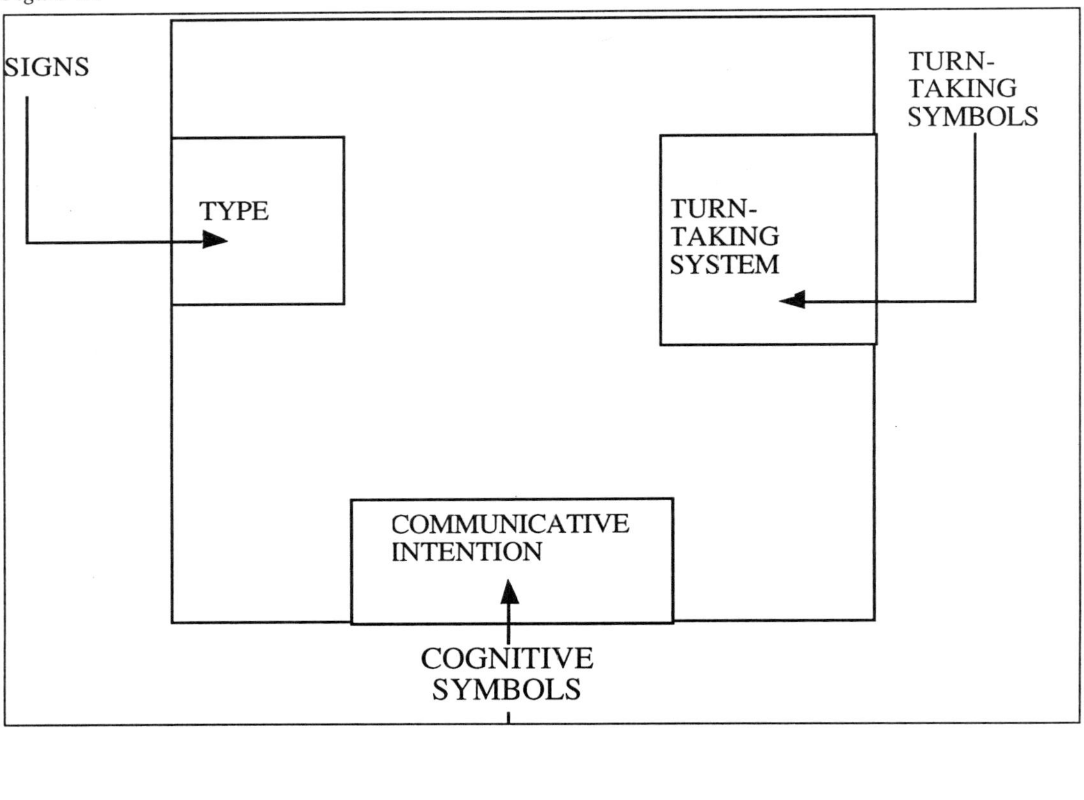

In other words it matters whether one takes Line A or Line B and the choice needs to be made explicit, from the beginning.

In some cases a high level of qualitative information may be useful while in others a lower level of qualitative information may be enough.

If one takes Line B, by adding qualitative information both on a global level (signs) and on local level (symbols), one may feel that general information (canvases) are no longer useful, because such information has been either explained more thoroughly or changed in the course of the process. A canvas may then be absorbed and the text may merely carry signs. There will be no loss in the qualitative information but more specific information.

Visual Text Programming

The use of CPP-TRS visual tools in text planning and processing can be defined as being transparent for two reasons:

1. The CPP-TRS visual tools and icons are kept visible, that is, transparent both to the visual text planner and the visual text processor.
2. The CPP-TRS visual tools and icons make the text transparent by allowing the visual text planner to show what he/she has planned the text to be and the visual text processor to see what would otherwise have been invisible or subject to arbitrariness.

Textual canvases, textual signs and textual symbols represent qualitatively different instructions for the visual text planner and therefore convey qualitatively different messages to the visual text processor. They are tools for making visible what is not visible in text at a purely linguistic level.

The textual canvases show how a text planner can visually plan and organize texts that have specific communicative purposes. Canvases help a text planner reflect on and visualize what he is doing as he prepares for and begins to organize a text.

CPP-TRS provides the text planner with visual tools that can integrate qualitative reasoning about text within the text itself. The textual signs provide a text with the additional possibility of explaining the communicative function of a text or a part of a text. They tell text processors on a global level what text is about, before they get to the language of the text. These signs are therefore more immediate and less abstract than the textual symbols.

Textual symbols enhance the communication between the text planner and the text processor. These symbols raise the semantics of text by making communicative intentions explicit. By using these symbols a text planner makes more evident to himself what he is trying to accomplish in the text he is planning.

There are two kinds of textual symbols. The first kind characterizes the style or type of text, while the second kind facilitates an interaction between the text planner and the text processor.

CPP-TRS Visual Programming

A CPP-TRS-based visual programming of text is founded on a highly skilled interpretation process as icons and schemes represent interpretative processes acting on natural language and on text configuration.

Pictorial representation and pictures in general are most effective in programming, as pointed out by Shu (1988):

1. Pictures are more powerful than words as a means of communication; they can convey more meaning in a more concise unit of expression.
2. Pictures aid understanding and memory.
3. Pictures may provide an incentive for learning to program a text.
4. Pictures do not have language barriers and if they are properly designed can be understood by all people, regardless of the language they speak.

Visual text programming, reframed in CPP-TRS terms, uses meaningful graphic representations in the process of programming a text, where programming means specifying a method for explaining those interpretative cues that will allow any consistent text operations to take place.

It is important to remember that even if our minds have powerful recognition capabilities, they are still susceptible to information overload. It is very important that the graphics are not so overwhelming that they can no longer be processed effectively.

It is evident that the CPP-TRS model is intended to raise the semantics of text as well as to facilitate text planning, organizing, structuring and processing by making available some commonly shared visual tools that represent and indicate specific operations.

Terms such as writer or reader, sender or receiver, have therefore been redefined as visual text planner and visual text processor sharing the consensual system.

Conclusion

CPP-TRS is a new paradigm. It reverses the traditionally accepted way of looking at text structuring "bottom up" by creating a multiple view of text that is "top down".

Visual tools and icons are not intended to be a substitute for words or sentences; they are rather intended to represent invisible aspects of language so they may be added to text, thereby raising the level of the semantics.

Visual text planning (writing) and visual text processing (reading) may therefore be conceived as extensions of the traditional way of looking at text production and text understanding, by providing a consensual visual system for facilitating both processes in a transparent and cognitive way.

A CPP-TRS-Based Environment for Operating Text

Introduction

Operation research is the application of a scientific method to the management of organized systems.

The three essential characteristics of operation research are system orientation, use of interdisciplinary teams, and the adaptation of the scientific method to the conditions under which the research is conducted.

A crucial aspect of operation research is model construction. Symbolic models are completely abstract and when the symbols in a model are defined, the model is given content or meaning. A system that has the same structure as another, however different the two may be in content, can be used as a model of the other. Such a model is called an analogue.

A CPP-TRS environment for organizing high quality, high speed information is presented here. The same environment will be considered as a guide to the exploration of the structure of the problem identified in order to reveal possible courses of action.

On Text Operations

Whenever we talk or write, or more generally, organize language structures in order to be able to communicate, that is, convey knowledge based on certain intentions, we create texts. CPP-TRS (Tonfoni, 1989-94) is an integrated environment based on a well-defined and multilayered visual system with different levels of complexity specifically intended to represent and highlight those different cognitive processes that occur when a text is structured. These are called text operations. A text needs to be considered both on a global level and on a more local one. Operating a text implies controlling the text itself at different levels. Control on a global level means being able to identify the communicative function of a certain text, whereas control on a local level means being able to distinguish the communicative intention that occurs at the paragraph or even at the sentence level.

From a CPP-TRS perspective both the writer of the text, also called the sender, and the reader of the text, also called the receiver, can be defined as text operators (TO).

CPP-TRS can be productively used to identify and visually represent the text operator's global and local patterns of communication. A global communicative pattern (GCP) means the overall communicative function of a text. A local communicative pattern (LCP) means the intention of the paragraph or sentence as well as the turn-taking that may be requested of another text operator. In some ways communicative patterns are more important than words and sentences because they actually control meaning at a higher level. They are usually apprehended only after processing and interpreting the whole text, which involves time and effort on the text operator's part and many arbitrary decisions. In many cases, they are missing altogether because even the text operator may not be able to define them if he/she has not become aware of them.

CPP-TRS is a well-defined visual organization system that is as consistent as and no less significant than the system of punctuation.

In order to be able to operate text consistently, text operators will have to share the operation system both at the level of text production and at the level of text understanding. From a CPP-TRS perspective, text production is defined as text actualization (TA) whereas text understanding is defined as text sensing and perceiving (TSP). To analyze the overall process let us now look at the global dynamic scheme, which represents a CPP-TRS based environment for operating text (fig. 5.1).

First we should observe that the text operator or crew of text operators is placed in the centre of the environment to indicate that this is where the global control is located. In other words, the control of the overall process both at a local and at the global level is with the text-operators' crew (TOC). Now let us proceed stage by stage through the different positions:

Position 1 (information flow): when open, the information flow, made of unprocessed sequences of information, is activated; its basic unit is the Information Flow Unit (IFU) which has not yet been processed. The information flow will undergo a process of texture configuration organized by the text-operators' crew, which means that there will be a visualization of information distribution, made possible by the activation of texture detectors (CPP-TRS canvas) by the text-operators' crew.

Position 2 (information texture): once configured the information texture can be subdivided into Information Texture Units (ITU). This is the departure point for text actualization.

The text actualization process suggests that the text-operators' crew, who have been monitoring the texture configuration process, will be able to convert the information texture, that is those ITU that have been chosen, into an actual text. In order to turn the non-actualized texture into an actual text, the text-operators' crew will have to activate both text sensors (CPP-TRS signs) and text perceptors (CPP-TRS symbols).

Position 3 (actual text): once actualized, the text shows the active sensors and perceptors, which act as macro-instructions (sensors) to extract the GCP from the text and as micro-instructions (perceptors) to extract the LCP from the text. As a result of the consensually shared system, text sensors will be able to produce text sensing and text perceptors will be able to produce text-perception. Text sensing means that the text-operators' crew will be able to recognize the GCP within the text, indicated by the CPP-TRS signs system. Text perception means that the text-operators' crew will be able to recognize LCP within the text, indicated by the CPP-TRS symbols system.

CPP-TRS visually processed text units are also defined as Communicative Patterns Units (CPU), which incorporate text and both sensors and perceptors. This means that each CPU is transparent to any text operator based on the same system of representation.

The actual text may undergo a further process of reformulation which means that each CPU may be expanded into a virtual communicative space.

Such process is made possible by using and applying the CPP-TRS and is called text virtualization.

The text-operators' crew will then operate on text-sensors by modifying their communicative function (trajectory). A sensor that is being modified in its original trajectory is named text effector. The text-operators' crew may also operate on text perceptors by modifying their communicative intention and turn-taking (energy). A perceptor that is being modified in its original energy is named a text manipulator. The result of such set of operations is a virtual text.

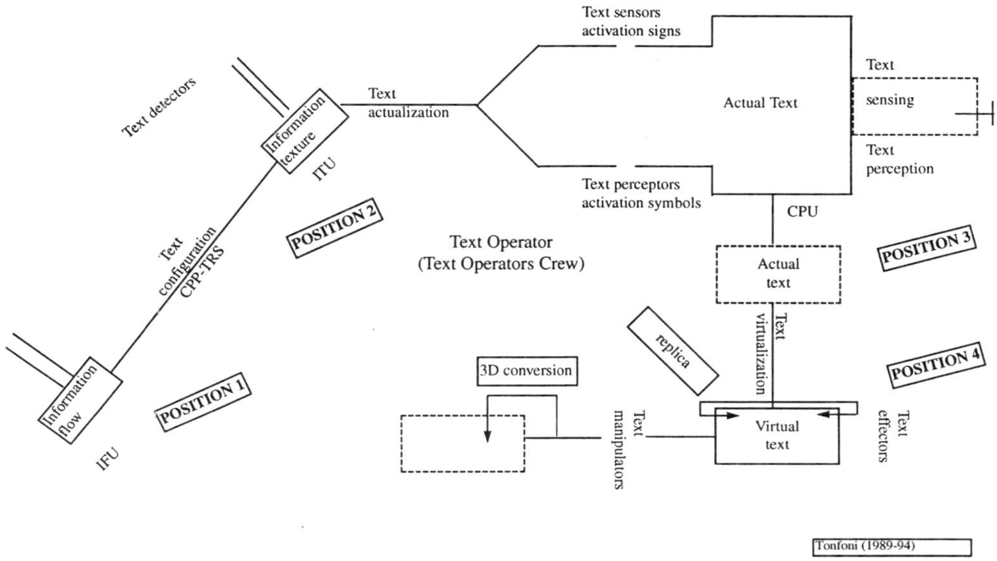

Figure 5.1

Position 4 (virtual text): Once virtualized, the text shows both the active effectors and the manipulators, which act as macro-instructions (effectors) to modify the GCP of the actual text, and as micro-instructions (manipulators) to modify the LCP of the actual text.

As a result of the consensually shared system, text effectors and text manipulators will be able to modify (virtualize) text sensing and text perception.

A virtualization process where text effectors and text manipulators are active can be defined as a multilayered conversion.

There is one more possibility in virtualizing text which is to amplify it into a 3-D communicative space. Such process is called 3-D conversion and it is activated by text amplifiers (CPP-TRS textual objects and machines).

To summarize, we can say that text virtualization means the following:

The text operator, after having sensed and perceived the actualized text, will decide to operate on the patterned and perceived text to extend it into a communicative environment other than that in which it exists by applying CPP-TRS and leaving it transparent. Text virtualization means that he creates different communication spaces for an actualized text which becomes a virtual text with a set of visible operations. It is very important to distinguish between information texture which is not virtual but potential and not yet actualized, and virtual text which is an extension and expansion of an actualized text within a virtual space of communication.

Let us now go back to the overall process represented in Figure 5.1. This shows that a text operator or a crew of text operators may act at different stages but keep overall control based on a mutual and consensual sharing of the CPP-TRS system.

The behaviour of a text operator affects the communicative environment.

Since the text operator may exhibit many kinds of communicative behaviours, it is very important to be able to recognize and name them consistently in order to have transparency and over all control.

This is why CPP-TRS (Tonfoni, 1989-94) promotes self-awareness in each individual (TO), in a crew (TOC) and within a more extended communicative environment (CPP-TRS-based environment).

We all know that the punctuation system allows the reader to distinguish an interrogative sentence from a declarative one. In a similar way, by self-reflecting on communicative behaviour the text operator will be able to identify and use an appropriate visual representation provided by CPP-TRS in order to make GCP and LGP explicit. In some ways, CPP-TRS can be defined as a communicative traffic control system enhancing the active role of the text operator. As with any system, by knowing the basic rules, an infinite number of operations may be performed and understood in a quick, unambiguous and easy way. CPP-TRS allows any text operator to actualize any kind of text by following very simple instructions leading to more complex explanations. By conveying GCP and LCP visually, even interactions occurring in different languages at the same time can be facilitated.

The whole CPP-TRS system is based on the concept that you can enhance and mutually control communication by visually processing text. The starting point is a visible global organization of text, and the ending point is the actual language of the text. This approach is soundly grounded in cognitive research that is explicitly aimed at explaining the complexities of how our minds apprehend, process and communicate knowledge.

Figure 5.2.

CPP-TRS is for:

Improving textual resolution
Promoting active sensing and perception
Enhancing visualization of information distribution
Increasing speed of knowledge processing
Increasing reliability in positioning detection by communicative pattern recognition
Increasing reliability in information structuring active text sensing and perception

CPP-TRS is also for:

Active processing and utilization of information redundancy
Active processing and utilization of contradictory information
Active extraction of abstractive knowledge
Active high speed and high accuracy sensing and perception
Active knowledge acquisition and noise reduction
Active processing of uncertain information and solving of ill-posed problems
Active determination of sensing and perception strategies.

CPP-TRS (Tonfoni, 1989-94)

On Implementing CPP-TRS-Based Solutions

Let us now move into a more detailed description of the different components of CPP-TRS by first identifying the overall purpose of CPP-TRS, which is presented in Figure 5.2.

In CPP-TRS there is no such thing as mere language organization, where words and sentences flow out automatically and unambiguously convey intention and meaning, because this does not actually happen. There is rather a process of communicative labelling that makes transparent those aspects of language that are most difficult to represent, which is what actually happens in communication.

Language is very complex. For example, it is very difficult to understand from the sentence "It's cold in here. The window is open" the message "Please close the window". There is no evidence for it whatsoever in the language itself. There is simply no direct link between words, meaning, function, intention and turn-taking. This is the kind of ambiguity we find all the time, because it is implicit in language as a communicative system.

In CPP-TRS, the traditional process of text production is reversed. Instead of starting with words, the producer of a text must first understand his/her own intention, then design the structure of the text, and finally select words and sentences for it. This approach avoids the pitfalls of the traditional approach by making communicative intentions explicit at the very beginning.

Let us now have a look at the different CPP-TRS components shown in Fig. 5.3.

The system is being used by the text-operators' crew in a transparent way. The transparent use of the CPP-TRS system includes the visual representation of signs and symbols in the text so that the text-operators' crew can share tasks by mutually and consensually referring to a common system.

Now let us consider the CPP-TRS activated system both in text actualization and in text virtualization by looking at Fig. 5.4.

What has been described up to now is an overall view of a CPP-TRS based environment for operating text at different levels and in different stages.

Fig. 5.3 — Visual text actualization, sensing and perception

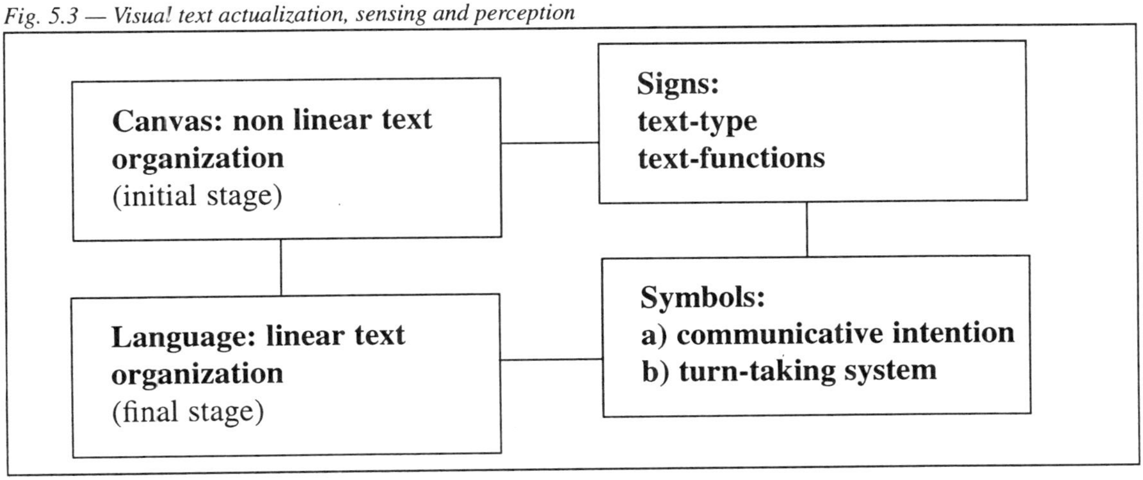

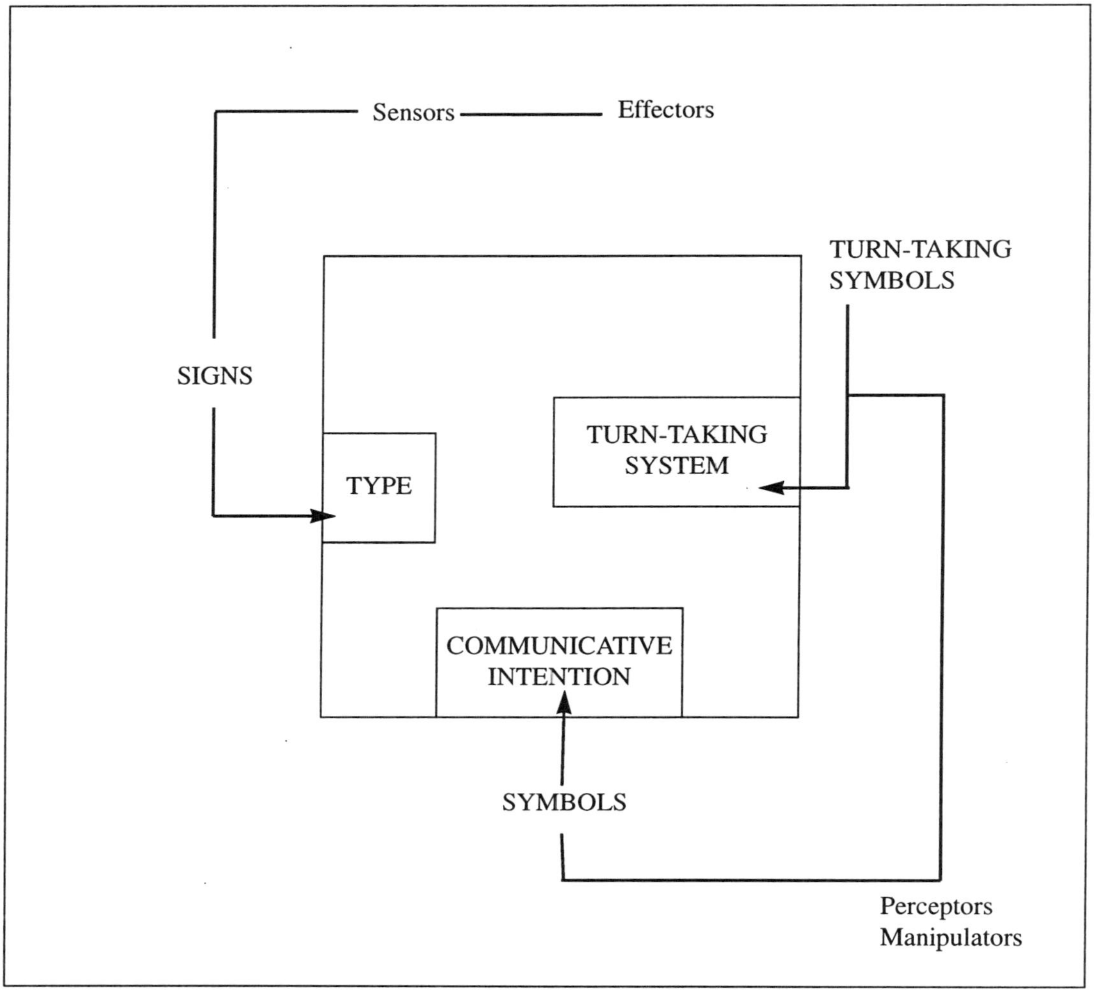

Figure 5.4 — Text Actualization [sensors] [perceptors] – Text Virtualization [effectors] [manipulators]

The text operator or text-operators' crew is designed to play an active role in the overall process through a defined set of active communication displays.

Through the different components of the CPP-TRS-based environment, we can describe the design of a multilayered tool for information detection and transformation, called a CPP-TRS active information scanner, which can be activated in positions 3 and 4 of the CPP-TRS environment for operating text. The active scanner design can be seen in Figures 5.5 and 5.6.

Conclusion

We can conclude that CPP-TRS is both a methodology and a language. Through the CPP methodology (Tonfoni, 1989-94) those invisible aspects of communication are identified and represented by the TRS metalanguage, which complements natural language.

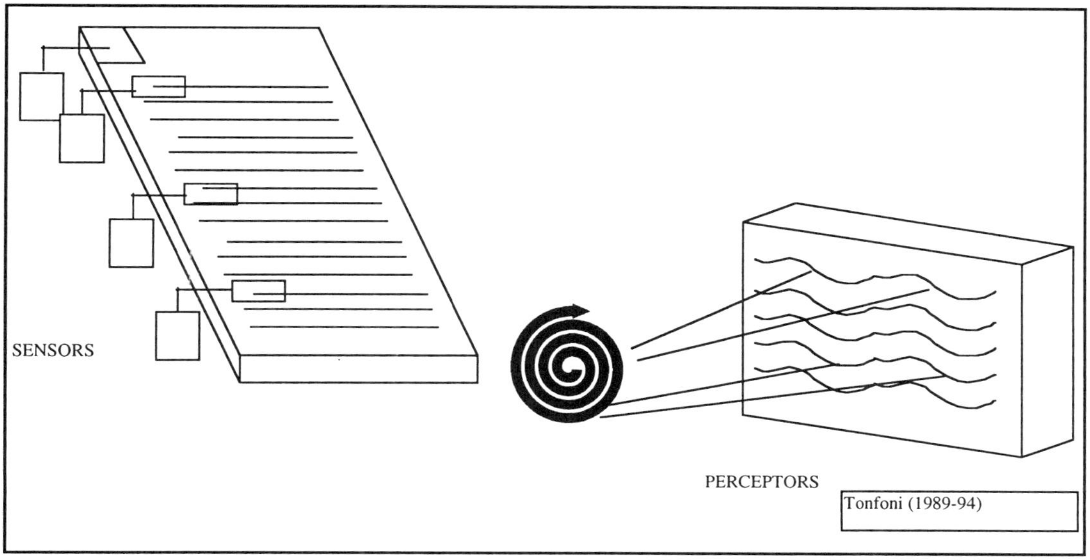

Figure 5.5

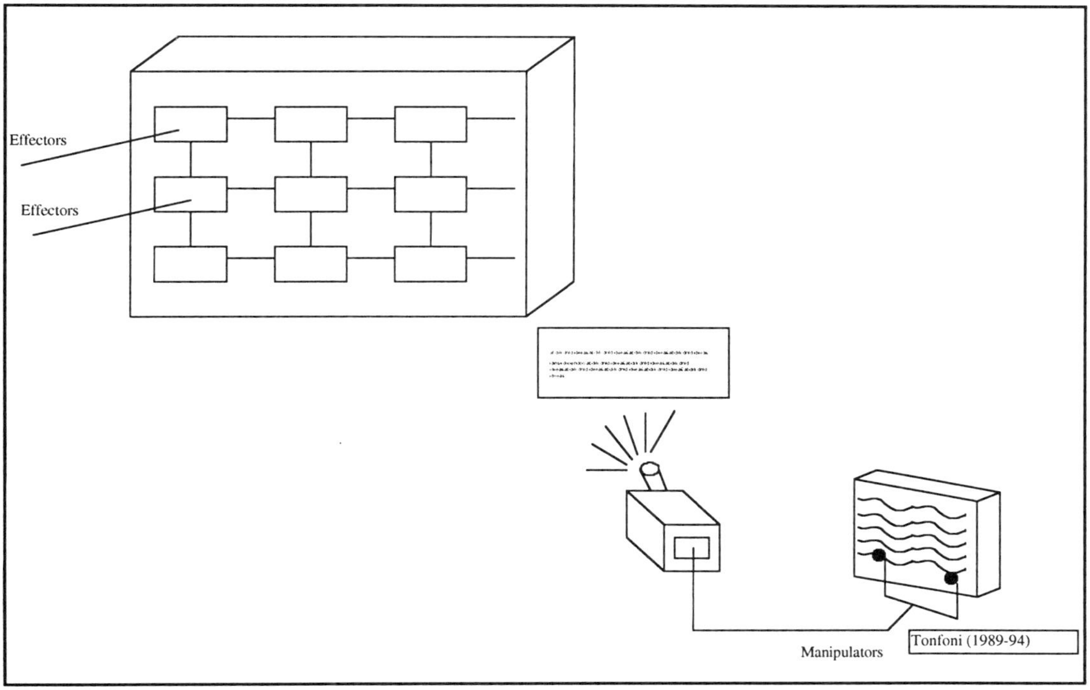

Figure 5.6

As a language by itself, CPP-TRS can be applied to a variety of fields.

A CPP-TRS-based E-Mail System Architecture

Introduction

A new model for conceiving and organizing e-mail is presented here. Based on a definition of qualitatively different categories of messages and networking attitudes, a CPP-TRS-based multiple tasks and multiple viewing architecture is illustrated.

CPP-TRS (Tonfoni, 1989-94) can be defined as a communicative traffic control system aimed at facilitating message production and delivery by visually pre-interpreting the message. As in any language, by knowing the syntax an infinite number of sentences can be generated, processed and understood in a quick, unambiguous and natural way. CPP-TRS allows the user to generate any kind of message from very simple information to more complex information storage, filing updating and forwarding.

In the present chapter only those visual schemes and tools of CPP-TRS will be presented that are directly relevant for the basic actions and processes that take place in e-mail.

Communicative Semantics of a Text

CPP-TRS is based on the concept that communication may be enhanced by visually perceiving text. The starting point is a visible global organization of text, and the ending point is the actual language of the text. This approach is soundly grounded in cognitive research that is explicitly aimed at explaining activities going on in the mind (Minsky, 1986; Schank, 1988). What is intended by "communicative semantics of a text" is the following kinds of information about the text, which can be organized at four different levels:

First level: global communicative plan of the text, which involves the kinds of operations and actions that work on a cognitive level to begin organizing a specific text.

Second level: global communicative function of the text, which is the overall typology of the text, and the kind of communicative functions the text is supposed to play.

Third level: local communicative intention of the different parts of the text, which means the variety of intentions and styles that can be found in each sentence or paragraph.

Fourth level: local communicative turn-taking of different parts of the text, which means that parts of the text may explicitly require some change or update on the text-receiver's part according to a request made by the text-producer.

Communicative semantics is therefore a qualitative description of quantitative information, whereby qualitative description, communicative function, intention and turn-taking are considered and quantitative information sentences and paragraphs are as well.

CPP-TRS is therefore an unambiguous, quick, and effective system for reinforcing natural language use in e-mail and networking, as it is a communication traffic control system designed to facilitate text production, delivery, interpretation, passing, filing and retrieving.

As has been previously mentioned, CPP-TRS consists of two integrated parts. CPP stands for Communicative Positioning Program, and is the methodological component of the system. The CPP methodology enables the receiver to understand how the sender has positioned himself/herself with regard to certain information. It is a complete programme that provides visual schemes, models, and tools to organize information effectively.

TRS stands for Text Representation Systems and is the visual language component. It is strictly integrated within the CPP methodology and is the corresponding way of representing those cognitive processes and communicative actions that have been identified by CPP.

CPP-TRS starts from a global perspective, reflecting visually the communicative intention and function of a message (type) as well as the role the receiver should play by receiving and returning the message.

CPP-TRS provides the user with the set of visual tools that are suited to structuring text and communicating effectively.

The CPP-TRS Model and the various applications of it (Tonfoni, 1989-94) have been thoroughly analyzed and illustrated in much detail in the literature.

Just as an artist chooses a canvas with an appropriate texture, a sender needs to decide how much "texture of information" the text will have. The texture of text has to do with the density of information conveyed by it and depends on the particular communicative purpose of the text. Before organizing a message, the sender prepares for it by thinking about the text. Text can be written from a multitude of perspectives and points of view, with many different focuses, intentions and organizational considerations. Each way of writing text enables a different viewing of it and is an invitation to the writer to "redraw" it.

Visual symbols are like road signs that tell a driver what lies ahead or like the notation that directs a musician to play a movement slowly and softly or briskly and lively; they enhance the communication between the sender and the receiver of text. These symbols raise the semantics of text by making its meaning explicit. By using these symbols a sender makes more apparent to himself and to his receivers what he is trying to accomplish in the text he writes.

In e-mail applications, the first kind of symbols characterize the style or type of message, while the second kind facilitate an interaction between the sender and receivers of text. The text-style symbols are describe, define, narrate, point out, explain, regress, reformulate, synthesize, analyze, express.

These text symbols are named as verbs, whose precise meanings are based on ancient Latin words that carry strong suggestions about the cognitive process the symbols represent. For instance, describe comes from the Latin word "describo", which means to write about or write around in a free, unconstrained manner. A description can provide as much or as little information as the writer chooses, and it does not need to be put in a logical or chronological order.

The text symbols are designed so that they intuitively convey the intention of the text with which they are associated. For example, the symbol for describe is a spiral with an arrow on the outer end and conveys the free, unconstrained characteristics of a description. Text symbols control text locally.

A second set of symbols are the turn-taking symbols. A sender can place turn-taking symbols within the message to facilitate a dialogue with the receivers of the message. These symbols explicitly tell the receivers how the sender wants them to interpret the message and when it is their turn to take part in modifying it.

Signs in CPP-TRS (Tonfoni, 1989-94) control the text on a global level. They tell readers on a global level what the text is about, even before the readers begin to read the language of the text. These signs are therefore more immediate and less abstract than the visual symbols.

As in a polittico painting, a sender can shape, partition and organize text to help receivers visually understand its main focus. The sender can put textual elements together so that the arrangement itself emphasizes what is central and what is peripheral — that is, what is most important and what is less important, but still relevant. The different shapes of the textual elements can, moreover, provide multiple views of the text as a whole, to enable readers to comprehend it in all its complexity, and possibly choose and substitute other texts.

In order to plan an overall e-mail system architecture to provide message packaging, filing, storage, retrieval and delivery based on CPP-TRS, it is important to think about different tools with their different purposes.

Users may be merely readers or active commentators; the key role is played by the user who is perhaps better called the chooser, of those different tools that are available.

The user has therefore been redefined in CPP-TRS as the chooser to underline the active role he/she is supposed to play both in deciding the kind of communicative tasks he/she is addressing and the kind of tools he/she will choose to operate.

CPP-TRS provides the chooser with a whole set of visual tools that have been conceived and planned to structure text according to an extremely powerful communicative semantics, which allows the text to convey visually those aspects of language that are not conveyed linguistically.

In CPP-TRS the message organizer will be able to process and make transparent those aspects that are most difficult to grasp and therefore to transmit.

The CPP-TRS e-mail thus will provide the chooser with a set of visual tools, shown in Figure 6.1, that are specifically suited to structuring text and communicating it effectively.

What Figure 6.1 shows are the different kinds of visual tools provided for the chooser to organize the communicative semantics of his messages by raising the visual perception of his text.

Starting at the canvas, which is intended to represent the global communicative plan of the text (first level of Communicative Semantics), the chooser moves on to signs, which represent the global communicative function of the text (second level of Communicative Semantics).

After signs, the chooser finds two kinds of symbols representing local communicative intentions (third level of Communicative Semantics) and local communicative turn-taking respectively (fourth level of Communicative Semantics).

Finally and as the end result of the previously organized levels, the chooser moves to a linear organization of the text.

A large and extremely interesting literature on e-mail has explored inter-

Figure 6.1

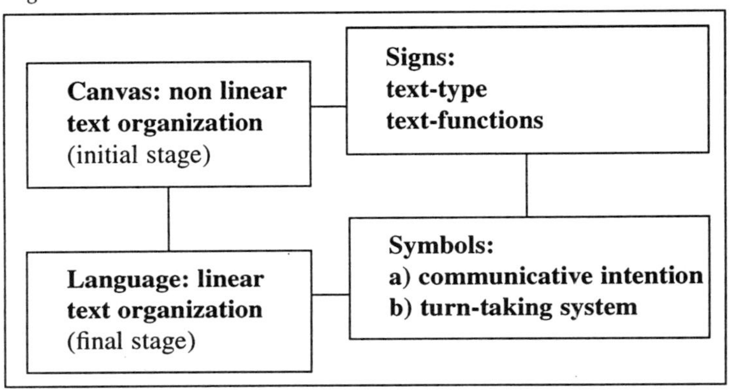

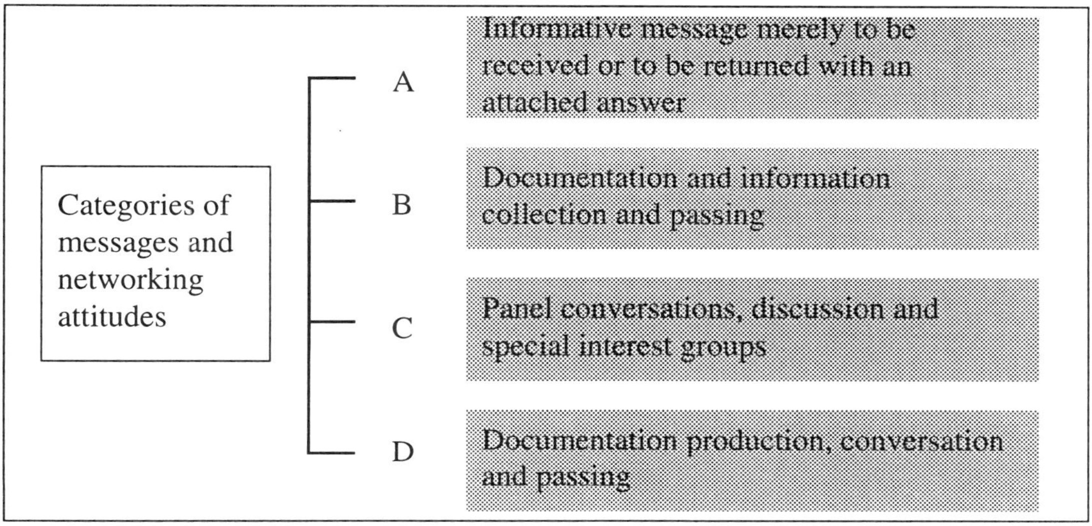

Figure 6.2

networking and organization problems at various levels (Ginsberg, 1986; McQuillan and Walden, 1977, Partridge, 1986, 1988; Tannenbaum, 1988).

A CPP-TRS E-mail System

The CPP-TRS approach to e-mail system architecture is based on the identification of a set of qualitatively different communicative actions that refer to message categories and the corresponding networking attitudes. Message is defined as "that text or text unit which is meant to move from a certain original location to another targeted one or more and which leaves a trace in the original location (copy) or comes back partially or totally modified in one or more stages. The message is subject to change, revision, multiple agent bunching."

The categories of messages that correspond to qualitatively different attitudes to networking are represented in Figure 6.2.

Let us now specify more precisely the kinds of communicative actions that are actually involved in each of these categories:

A. By informative messages production and delivering, which is merely received or returned with a simple answer we mean meetings, announcements, single appointments, single news items or updating. Such messages usually move from an individual who takes responsibility and initiative to another individual or individuals.

B. By documentation and information collecting and passing is meant the conversion of personal files into public documents. The process originates with individuals but is extended to a collective group. Everyone is able to contribute by expanding the text quantitatively, that is by adding more information, and qualitatively by changing the qualitative aspect of the text. Information and documentation collecting and passing usually moves from single individuals to the group.

C. By panel conversations, discussions and special interest groups is intended those groups of individuals who are linked together by common tasks or interests and act in

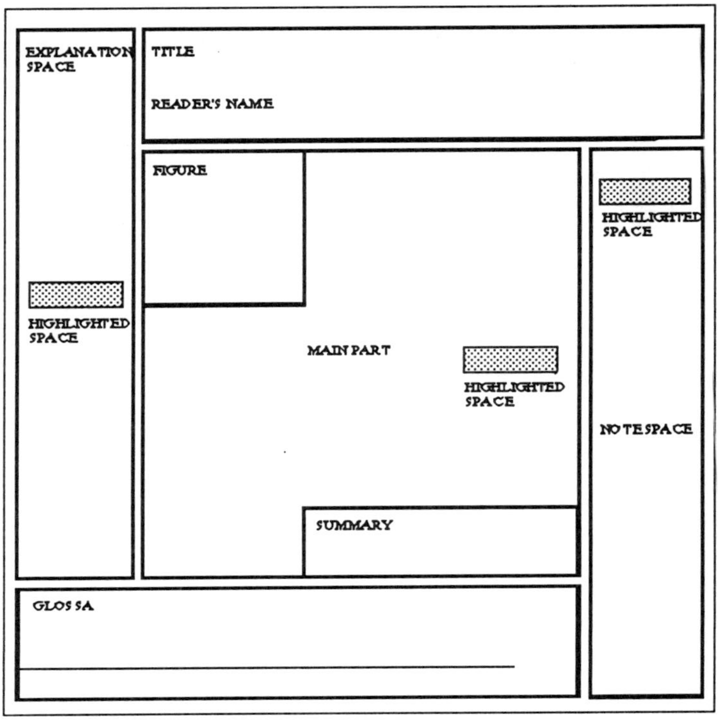

Figure 6.3 — Textual Miniature structure

groups by playing specific roles, which may change over time but can always be identified. Texts that are produced or passed may be collective news or comment on topics raised and discussed. The group is organized and assisted by a facilitator, who assigns tasks as well as directs the overall action by assigning turns to participants.

D. By documentation production, conversion and passing what is meant is the conversion of existing documents as well as updating and revision. It involves groups of individuals who cooperate by exchanging roles but are still able to keep track of the kind of communicative operations that are performed on a qualitative level. A directive role needs to be played by someone, even if this is done on a turn-taking basis and is temporary.

The chooser who organizes the Informative Message [Category A] is provided with two specific CPP-TRS visual tools: the Textual Miniature and the Canvas for Text Rotation.

Let us look at the Textual Miniature. A Textual Miniature is a visual tool for both the individual and collective organization of information to be sent or expanded and completed.

In the CPP-TRS-based e-mail system a Textual Miniature is suited to the circulation of information on a one-to-one basis. The message sent may also be collective, but it originates with one person and is disseminated to several receivers.

The Text Miniature is based on a consistent text-partitioning map on the text-space. The text-partitioning map defines text "islands" that contain different kinds of information as shown in Figure 6.3.

The main part of the text space contains what the sender plans as the common and shared part of the text. The other parts of the text space have different communicative functions. The upper part contains the topic and the receiver's name and may also present the perspective suggested to the receiver. The topic islands may also contain specific requests for completion.

The sender may ask the receiver to add some information or merely to acknowledge receipt: some parts of the text may also be highlighted so that the receiver may focus on

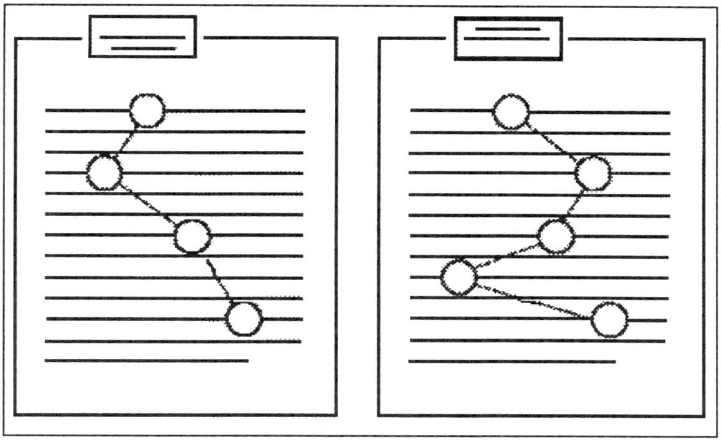

Figure 6.4. Canvas for Text Rotation

them. Once highlighted, the receiver may transfer, repeat or headline a word or sentence on a side-island note space. The note space, which adds to or expands the information in the main text, will appear on the right side of the main text, since it is intended to be read after it.

A word or sentence may also be highlighted, transferred, repeated and headlined on another side-island, which is called the explanation space.

The explanation space is intended to provide more information in the form of causal explanation, including the reason something happened, an additional justification or some background information. This space will appear on the left side of the main text, because the sender may like to read it before the main text. The summary space is located at the bottom of the main text; and will contain a summary of the main points or facts that have been presented in the main text.

The glossa space completes the text-organization space and appears below the summary space. It may contain comments of the sender but may also be completed by the receiver. The communicative interaction obtained by text-miniaturing in CPP-TRS is one-to-one and is directed and controlled by the sender; which means that the sender will receive complete messages back from each of the respective receivers.

The receivers fill up different spaces according to the sender's specific request but they do not necessarily know each others' responses.

A Canvas for Text Rotation is suited for the production of many slightly differing messages at the same time.

Rotating text is concerned with organizing texts that carry the "same" message to receivers who have qualitatively and quantitatively different information needs. When rotating a text, the sender concentrates on presenting information in ways that take into account a specific reader's viewpoint. Fig. 6.4 shows a visual representation of text rotation.

In order to help a chooser collect information, turn it into a document and pass it [Category B], a specific visually organized CPP-TRS tool is provided, the Functionalized Textual Origami.

Rather than considering text in traditional page-oriented amorphous fashion, CPP-TRS challenges the chooser to think of text as having a shape. The specific shape given to text visually and explicitly conveys its meaning to receivers. Text can be square, triangular, semicircular or some other shape; there is a syntax of textual shapes because each shape carries a specific communicative intention. Square-shaped text identifies the text as a story, triangular-shaped text tells you that it embodies a memory, and so on.

This syntax of shapes enables the construction of textual structures, as well as the

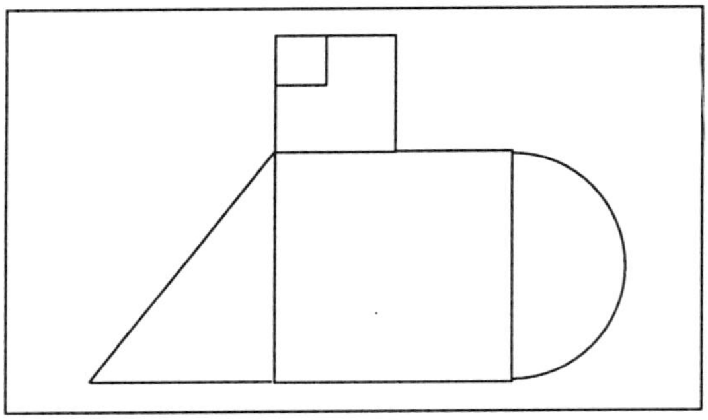

Fig. 6.5 — Functionalized Textual Origami

completion of a text. As a writer you can combine the various textual shapes together to create structures that resemble a textual origami. Receivers may also take their turn in shaping the text in their own ways and adding to the structure you present to them.

The text is shaped into various forms according to the specific function of the text. The shape of the text itself is therefore evidence of the communicative intention so that receivers immediately know the intention.

CPP-TRS provides a set of two-dimensional geometric signs to shape text. Textual signs are like traffic signs whose specific shapes immediately and unambiguously alert the receiver.

An example of a textual origami to be filled up with functionalized texts or text units is shown in Figure 6.5.

The sender will be able to organize different parts of the text so that the arrangement itself emphasizes what is central and what is peripheral. The different shapes of the textual elements also provide multiple views of the text as a whole, enabling receivers to comprehend it in all its complexity and, possibly, choose, add, substitute or take away other texts.

To help groups of individuals who share the same interest to hold panel discussions, by alternating roles [Category C], a specific CPP-TRS visual organization is provided, called the Textual Polittico.

A polittico has a central space containing the main subject and a set of complementary parts that can be opened or closed, like doors.

Figure 6.6 — Polittico (on the left) and trittico (on the right)

The simplified form of a polittico has three parts — the central, the main part and two lateral ones — and is called a trittico. Both polittico and trittico are shown in Fig. 6.6.

A Textual Polittico is particularly suited to text-space organization for raising and discussing a topic. A topic may be raised and receivers/panelists may be required to comment and visually organize their opinions which are then circulated as an expanded text. The open discussion on the topic can be expanded so that more and more receivers are put on the panel. The polittico is different from the miniature because all the individuals participating know each others' views and reactions to the topic. Moreover, all the parts of the polittico are filled up at a predetermined time so that it is possible to see the views together.

When a chooser initiates a conferencing session, he decides on a certain number of panelists, assign turns and establishes a deadline so that all the panels of the polittico are completed and viewed at the same time. The initial chooser is the one who raises the topic, but is not the only one receiving comments, as all panelists will know about each other, read each others' comments, communicate with each other and are aware of each others' respective opinions and perspectives.

The polittico is ideal for electronic conferencing among a defined number of panelists. A panel director assigns turns to the panelists and asks each of them to comment on a certain topic once. The panelists know that they have only one turn and are entitled to only one comment on the topic. All of the panelists' comments appear on the lateral sides of the polittico painting — none of them is omitted. The panelists also need to know that someone will value their opinions and draw final conclusions about the panel session. The summary is understood as a collectively directed summary.

A suitable text may be a controversial topic. It may involve making a decision, solving a problem or asking for opinions.

Panelists must be willing to take a position and make a contribution by stating their individual perspectives. If the panelists would rather debate the issue among themselves, then a polittico structure is not the most suitable form. Panelists need to be aware that their own text is to be a reaction or answer to some triggering issue. They then have to devote time to think about and organize their text to present their own position. The text will be read by other panelists, as well as reported and summarized in the summary space.

A polittico structure involves individually-driven collective text organization. Each panelist contributes individually — by giving his own personal opinion and by organizing his own text — to a common project. The panel initiator completes the panel with a collective summary, which is based on reading and interpreting the point of view of each of the panelists.

To assist a group of individuals producing or commenting on existing documents and passing it [Category D], a four-level visual CPP-TRS tool is provided, the Textual Tapestry.

A tapestry is a rich metaphor because it visually carries certain characteristics of collective text organization.

The density of a tapestry corresponds to the quantity of a collectively organized text. Before subdividing tasks, a group must consider how much it needs to be textually organized. Sometimes the quantity of text is externally imposed, such as a specific page limit for a proposal, while other times the quantity is decided by the group. Tapestry also exhibits a complexity of design.

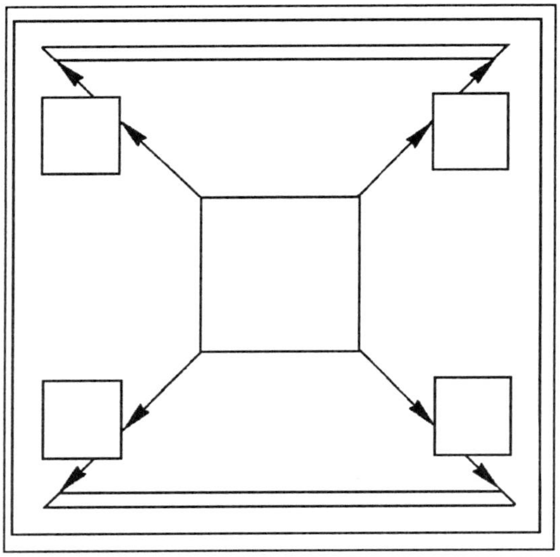

Figure 6.7 — Centrifugal model — start from the centre and go to the periphery

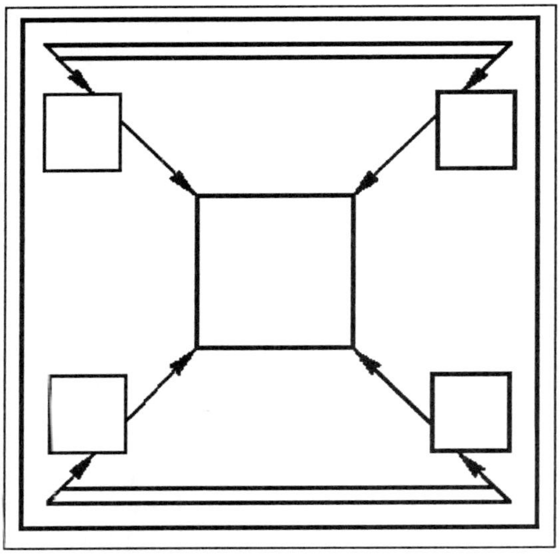

Figure 6.8 — Centripetal model — start from the periphery and move to the centre

Collective text organization is also complex and must be planned. Some products of a group effort are systematic and structured, while others are more open-ended and unstructured. Collective text organization always requires decision-making about who is going to take care of what and how the collectively organized text is going to come together. Collective text organization also requires cooperation among the group members to produce a shared product.

There are four visual models of tapestries that facilitate group interactions for collective text organization. Each visual model shows a different approach or attitude: the differences in these approaches are indicated visually by the way each model divides and defines space.

Let us now look at Figure 6.7.

The model in Figure 6.7 shows how a group can expand or revise a collectively written text. The text can be something like a report that needs to be updated. This text is represented by the large square in the middle. Arrows point outward from the central square to smaller squares around it. The smaller squares represent the new texts that result from the group's activity. The individuals in the group write these texts as a result of dividing the work and reflecting on or reacting to the original text.

The model is called centrifugal because the group starts from the central text and expands outward to texts written by the group members. This, of course, does not just happen. It must be planned so that the group members know what roles they have in the collective writing process. The group decides how the work will be divided and who will be responsible for writing each text.

The reverse of the centrifugal model is the centripetal model shown in Figure 6.8.

Centripetal means that the process of collective writing flows from the outside parts to the middle. In this model, the smaller squares around the outside represent existing texts.

These texts could be a set of individually prepared notes or memos about a certain topic. The group's job is to consider this material and integrate it into a collectively written text, which is represented by the large central square. As in the centrifugal model, the group plans how to integrate the material and makes decisions about the division of work among the group members.

What is interesting to note in both the centrifugal and centripetal models is that they preserve a record of the process of creating the collective text. In the centrifugal model, the existing central text remains with the individual texts triggered by it. Similarly, in the centripetal model the original texts are kept with the resulting integrated text.

This preservation of the process of collective text organization is important because it enables us to visualize the individual contributions, which will not get lost in the collective process.

The next two models represent a different approach to collective text organization. Figure 6.9 illustrates the linear rotation model.

In the linear rotation model the group is concerned with organizing a text that deals with a particular topic. Each group member decides to address the topic from the perspective of a particular communicative intention or point of view. For example, one member of the group may decide to organize a descriptive text, while another may want to organize an analytical text and give a more detailed explanation. Other members may choose to organize a topic from the perspective of their particular roles in the group or their viewpoints. What the group is doing at this point is deciding how to partition the space for organizing text. When the members finish their contributions, they are passed around and read.

Figure 6.9 — Linear rotation model — start from the upper left and proceed around the periphery clockwise

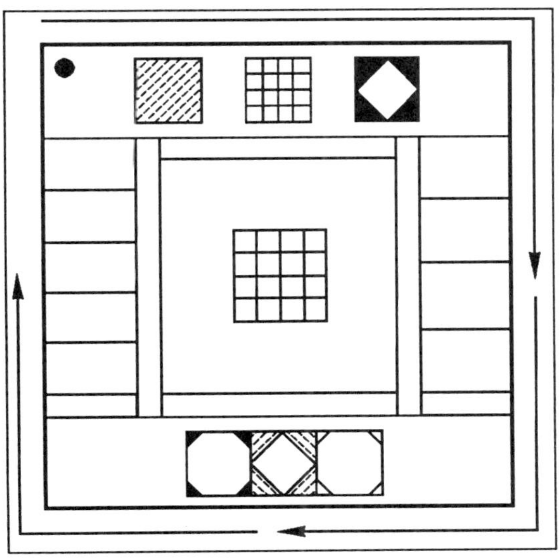

Figure 6.10 — Linear sequential model — start from the upper left and proceed across from left to right and then down

The patterns in the squares are all different because they represent the unique contributions of the members. Each contribution presents a specific point of view about the topic. These may be related to the different roles the members have or to the differences in their individual perspectives or feelings.

The group then considers each text in a linear fashion, moving around the square space of the visual model, as shown by the arrows. The group then decides which text seems the most relevant; the chosen text is considered the final written output of the group. This text is placed in the middle of the visual model as a representation of its importance.

Figure 6.10 shows the linear sequential model of collective text organization.

In this model the members of the group do not so much represent themselves as represent a collective thought. The group organizes a collective text. The texts contributed by the group members are represented by the rectangles. These texts, as in the linear rotation model, are read and discussed by the group. In this case, however, the order is linear sequential, going from left to right, top to bottom. Because the texts are the result of some other group process, they contain systematic, well-defined and accepted material.

Figure 6.11 — Canvas for collective text perception

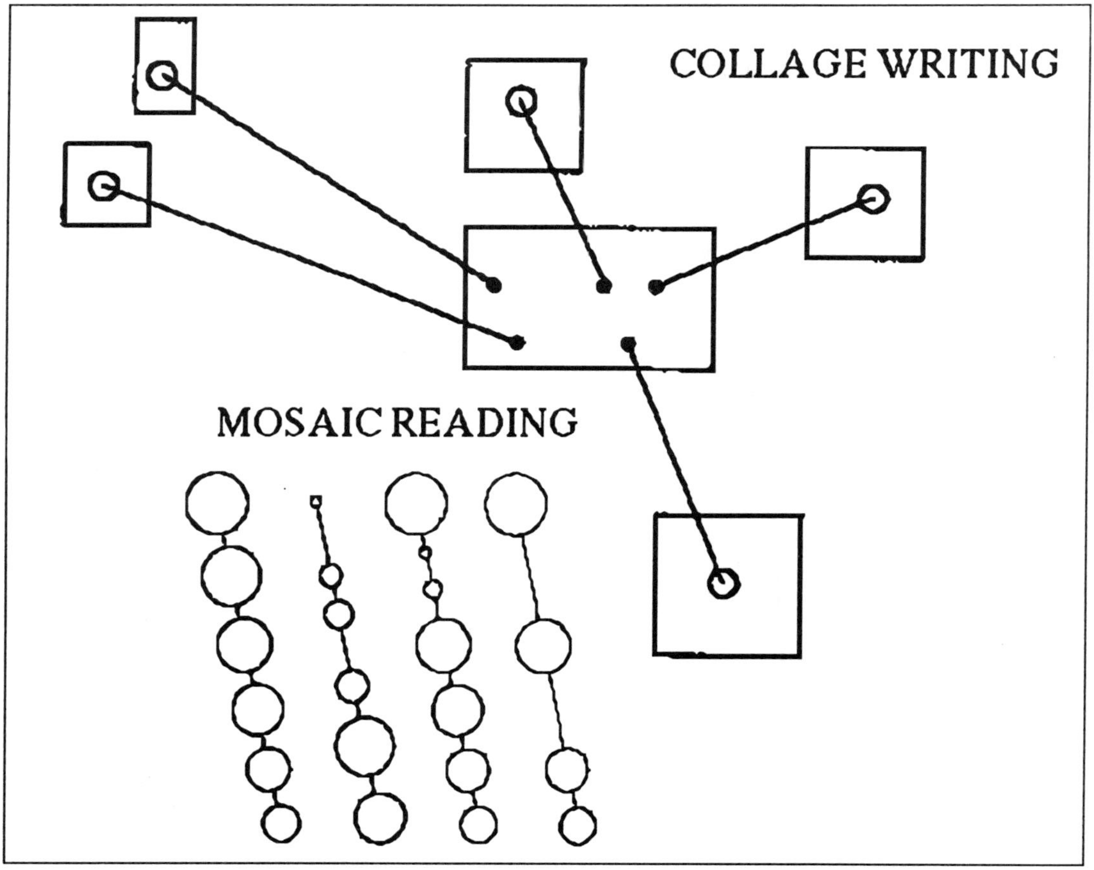

As the group discusses these texts, however, controversial issues may surface. Common concerns left undefined or that remain controversial are noted in the spiral motif by a word or short sentence. The group can then view these as questions, problems or issues needing resolution. They may become topics for further discussion.

To summarize, CPP-TRS asks the sender to start from a global perspective to reflect on the intention and function of each message. A set of "canvases" are provided. These are visual stimuli and global representations of communicative actions. Canvases are visual schemes that describe various communicative processes themselves and are navigation tools to guide the sender through the complexities of transmitting knowledge verbally.

Once the sender has a global view of what and how he/she is trying to communicate, he/she can then proceed to a more detailed structuring of texts. CPP-TRS provides visual signs and symbols for this.

Symbols are visual conventions that represent general types of text. Symbols represent communicative intentions and turn-taking.

CPP-TRS based visual aids of canvases, signs and symbols that are immediate, unambiguous and consistent can be used in combination according to the complexity of the message the sender is organizing.

One global metaphor that has turned into a specific canvas for collective text perception is the collage and mosaic. These visual schemes are intended to illustrate a collective perception experienced by a group of people writing or reading the same text asynchronously.

The first illustration in Figure 6.11 helps us visualize a particular type of collective writing defined as collage writing. Collage writing may be done by a group of people who collectively endeavour to create a text by piecing together their individual contributions.

Initially the group gets together to discuss the goal of the text, its style and the quantity of information they want it to contain. The members of the group then divide up the work. They discuss who is going to write each part of the text and how all parts fit together. This initial planning process is similar to what a group of architects do when planning the design of a house: the group decides who is responsible for designing the details of each room and makes sure that there is an overall plan so that the rooms fit together into one, unified structure.

Once the members of the group produce their individual texts, they meet to put these pieces together into a single text. This process is visually represented by the top illustration in Figure 6.11. The five smaller squares and rectangles surrounding the central, larger rectangle represent the text contributions of the individual members of the group. The central rectangle represents the text collectively written by the group.

The group writes the text from the texts contributed by the members. As in constructing a collage from various materials, the group cuts pieces of the texts provided by the members and pastes them into the new text they are creating. The way they do this may be somewhat unstructured.

The group thus creates the collectively written text from pieces of the individual texts of the members. This is illustrated in Figure 6.11 by the lines drawn from peripheral squares and rectangles to the central rectangle. The small circles within the peripheral squares and rectangles indicate that a piece of this text is cut. The point at which a line terminates within the central rectangle represents the place in the collectively written text where the cut texts are pasted. After the whole text is pasted together, the group then collectively reshapes it.

The illustration on the bottom side of Figure 6.11 represents mosaic reading. Mosaic reading shows how different readers can read the same text in different ways. In mosaic reading, a small group of people summarize the same text and then compare how their summaries differ. In the illustration, the line of connected circles at the far left represents the initial text that the group members read and summarize. The circles depict parts of the text, such as paragraphs. The size of the circles represent the relative importance or quantity of information intended and presented by the writer.

The three connected lines of circles to the right indicate how three different readers summarize the initial text. As in the representation of the initial text, the size of the circles indicates the relative importance that the reader gives to that part of the text in the summary.

The two illustrations in Figure 6.11 visually emphasize that a group of people perceive the same text differently. In collage writing, the collective perception of text is different from any one individual's perception of it. In mosaic reading, different readers perceive the same text in different ways. Because of these differences in text perception, it is extremely useful to offer guidance to help the reader perceive text the way it was intended. This is where the CPP-TRS signs and symbols come in. They indicate these aspects visually within the text and complement the language.

It is important to agree on the use of definitions such as "mosaic" and "collage", which are familiar terms but as used here are precise indications of specific textual operations. This ensures both transparency and evidence. As in a language, syntax needs to be known and respected if an infinite number of sentences are to be generated.

Conclusions

CPP-TRS (Tonfoni, 1989-94) is the basic structure, representing any communicative action taking place interlinguistically and interculturally. It is based on the idea of a shared consensual system that represents invisible aspects of natural language.

Given the qualitative differences of communication intentions carried through an e-mail system, CPP-TRS may be a tremendously powerful tool for message filing and retrieval. This is why different networking attitudes have been identified that correspond to different categories of message.

Notes

1. More extended description of textual polittico and textual tapestry may be found in Tonfoni G., *Writing as a Visual Art* (with James Richardson as Technical Writer and with a foreword by Marvin Minsky), 1994; first summarized English version of three previously published Italian books, respectively: *La scrittura multimediale* (1991), *La comunicazione come Arte Visiva* (1991), *Partitura Solfeggio Movimento* (1992).

Part Four

Introduction to Informactive Environments

Introduction: aims and intention

The aim of my research into communication is to help individuals communicate better by promoting a commonly shared "code".

Quality and effectiveness in communication are based on sharing and on respecting and valuing each individual's personal needs and preferences.

Technology today represents an extraordinary challenge but does not in itself guarantee that better communication will take place.

My intention has been to design new technological tools based on the responsible and active role of individuals. Therefore I have redefined some of the currently used terminology: for example, the user has become a chooser to underline that he or she will be in charge all the time; informative environments have become information active (informactive) environments because they are based on this new perspective on information processing, which is founded in transparency and active monitoring.

What is CPP-TRS? — basic information and some definitions

CPP-TRS (Communicative Positioning Program-Text Representation Systems) has been conceived, systematically designed and extensively tested by Tonfoni in the course of the last ten years. It is a cognitively based and therefore natural methodology and visual language using a system of 12 canvases, 10 signals, 14 symbols and a whole set of dynamic visual schemes. CPP-TRS is based on the fact that every communicative action is the result of a set of cognitive processes and the whole system is based on the concept that communication can be effectively enhanced by first recognizing the cognitive processes that are involved and then visually representing them. Using a very simple syntax, CPP-TRS is capable of visually representing meaning and intention as well as communicative function.

These are the invisible aspects of natural language that are most relevant to understanding the global meaning of a text. CPP-TRS is an unambiguous, quick and effective system for reinforcing natural language in any kind of interaction between and among individuals, with or without technology. It complements natural language by adding certain important elements that are not explicitly represented by natural language itself.

These elements include communicative intention and communicative function of the text expressed by the sender, as well as the role the reader, that is, the receiver of the text, is supposed to play.

These aspects are invisible in natural language because neither specific words nor punctuation convey them sufficiently and unambiguously; they are therefore non-transparent. As a language and as a consistent and well-defined system, CPP-TRS can be applied to an extremely wide variety of fields in both a transparent and non-transparent way.

CPP-TRS has been illustrated, documented and taught by Tonfoni, who has also been testing it for many years. In the past five years she has also designed a wide range of applications for CPP-TRS.

CPP-TRS a flexible standard: explanation of an apparently contradictory statement

It may sound contradictory but it is not: CPP-TRS is a flexible standard: "flexible" in that it will adapt to any kind of information and communication needs and is transportable; "standard" in that it will serve as a commonly shared and agreed set of rules for both encoding and interpreting communication and packaging and decoding information. The tremendous challenge CPP-TRS offers and the reason it was conceived is to reproduce and use the same criteria for any kind of information and communication, inside and outside the technology. CPP-TRS can be compared to a language. Just as the syntax (the set of rules to be respected) in any language ensures that one will be understood, so one must acquire the basic and simple syntax of CPP-TRS.

With any language, once having acquired the syntax, you are then able to produce freely and creatively any sentence. Similarly, you can use CPP-TRS in the way you want, when you wish and whenever you think that transparency in communication, by raising the visual perception of your text, may be of significant help in ensuring that your message is understood the way you intended.

It is legitimate for a composer to let those who execute his music know how he would like his music to be executed. CPP-TRS (Tonfoni 1989-94) intends to transfer the same concept into communication via language: if you send a message, you may be misunderstood. You want to reinforce your message visually by indicating exactly what you mean. The reader of the message will then know the intention because it has been explicitly declared by using commonly shared and agreed icons.

CPP-TRS can be applied to any language; as such, it does not limit any language, but rather explodes the communicative potential of each language. In the same way you would never think of musical notation as a constraint on a musician.

Musical notation is an agreed upon and internationally accepted system, which ensures that music is still used. Not only are there no complaints about musical notation but everybody learns it and accepts either as a way to compose or execute music. Andante, Allegro, Maestoso are specifically defined terms which are originally Italian but are now international.

A is a specific notation no musician would object to. Let us now explain an apparent paradox by referring to music. Musical notation ensures that music will be executed or played in a certain way. It may therefore be defined as a standard and flexible interpreter based on a set of instructions. A musical score may be read without being executed because musical notation is also a recognisable code by itself. Thus the player may both read the music score and play it.

Just as a musical score is divided into parts, a CPP-TRS encoded text may be processed in its units. This is how a high compression device for text-processing has also been developed, having great relevance for information highways applications in text transport and high speed, high accuracy and high transparency in knowledge processing (CPTRU and CPP-TRS Clip-sheet).

Music can be understood worldwide; it is the most international language. Nevertheless each individual is allowed to perceive and enjoy it in the way he/she wants. CPP-TRS teaches one how to execute and play information and how to perform communication in a way that greatly resembles how music is learned and played.

Music may be executed by a large variety of instruments; it therefore constitutes a unifying code to be implemented through a variety of possible interpretations.

The CPP-TRS notation system allows each individual to compose his/her communication score that can be understood, interpreted and executed.

Sometimes old words are not adequate to talk about new things: metaphors may create a virtual reality for appropriate explanation.

CPP-TRS is a tremendously powerful tool for the improvement of information and knowledge processing based on communication transparency and favouring and valuing the individual's own unique and precious contribution. This is not a contradiction; it is the only possible foundation for a real growth in information and communication technology.

The CPP-TRS skilled communicator: a physician, a craftsman and a runner

Metaphors and examples are very useful in explaining new facts and situations. A set of metaphors is here presented that can define accurately what a CPP-TRS skilled communicator will look like and is able to do. A CPP-TRS skilled communicator has to cope with a complex set of communicative situations and a variety of languages, as well as with a much increased quantity of messages and information to be processed. He/she will be competent in communication and information processing, which will make him/her sensitive to each different communicative situation. Like a physician, the CPP-TRS skilled communicator will be able to diagnose each communicative situation, discover the specific nature of each communicative problem that arises and to identify the specific tools that will be the most appropriate and useful with which to operate.

Not only will the CPP-TRS skilled communicator be able to recognize different functions performed by different technologies, but he/she will be fully aware of the specific structural properties of the variety of codes being used.

Each code has different properties: natural language may be extremely good for some purposes but not so good for others; icons may be appropriate in some situations but not in others. A CPP-TRS skilled communicator will know the structural properties of each code just like a craftsman knows and can recognize the physical properties of the material he/she is using.

A CPP-TRS skilled communicator will also progressively develop a sensitivity to information contexts, as well as to specific information needs shown by those individuals he/she is addressing; such sensitivity is based on the recognition of the different communicative patterns each individual shows in communicative performance. In order to recognize those "immaterial and invisible aspects of communication" which matter so much to understanding, mutual information exchange and negotiation, CPP-TRS will provide the communicator with a set of specifically designed techniques and a visual system of representation that will help him/her recognize, define and convey the most important aspects of a certain message, text, conversation or argument. A CPP-TRS skilled communicator will also be "cognitively skilled". What I mean by this is that in order to notice the different attitudes toward communication shown by individuals, it is important to recognize the current and common patterns which may then be referred to consistently.

To understand and recognize more fully the communicative patterns shown by others and to be able to adjust and syntonize, which constitutes the basis for respectful cooperation and a positive group-working attitude, the first step is to find out more about oneself by recognizing one's own cognitive tendencies and preferences that directly determine and characterize one's own ways of communicating. Through a "cognitive self-reflection process" the CPP-TRS skilled communicator will gain insight about himself/herself first in order to listen better and understand the other individuals' information needs and communication styles. Real effectiveness in communication is based on respect, recognition and appreciation of diversity as well. In order to become really aware of himself/herself on a cognitive basis, the CPP-TRS learning communicator will act a little like a competitive runner. He/she will be invited by the coach to slow down the process, observe the movement and reflect upon it, so that he can recognize it and see what happens; he/she will then be able to run again and much faster than before! What I am explicitly promoting is a cognitively based communicative awareness, which will then be transported by the CPP-TRS skilled communicator through the different media. What I intend to do is to link together an education process in advanced communication skills and information management to an active and effective use of advanced technology. My opinion, supported by evidence — I assume full responsibility for such a strong claim — is that this link is the only way to ensure enhanced and improved communication and information management today. A greater use of technology is not, by itself, a guarantee that the quality of communication and information processing will be increased. Communicators need to become skilled both at a technical level — which means that they need to know how to use the technology — and at a cognitive level — which means that they have to master different communication possibilities in a variety of different contexts and situations. To do this they need to develop their communicative competence, as a scientifically grounded, cognitively based, natural and practical skill.

CPP-TRS: a scientifically based and validated methodology for technical communication and documentation

CPP-TRS consists of two consistently integrated parts. CPP stands for Communicative Positioning Program and is the methodological component of the system. The CPP methodology enables communicators to understand how they position themselves in relation to their particular verbal and written communication. It is a complete programme that provides visual schemes, models, and tools to slow down the cognitive processes that are so vital in communication so that communicators may become aware of them and can control them to communicate effectively.

TRS, which stands for Text Representation Systems, is the visual language component. It is integrated with the CPP methodology and is an outgrowth of it. The CPP-TRS system encourages the communicator to start from a global perspective, to reflect on the intention and function of a written text. "Once the above communicator has a global view of what and how he/she is trying to communicate, he/she can then move to a more detailed structuring of the text. Advances in word-processing technology led Tonfoni to consider the possibility of moving text outside the flat space of a computer screen. The development of hypertext, with its concepts of levels or layers of text, further motivated her exploration of a physical, three-dimensional concept of text. The progress in artificial intelligence and cognitive science, moreover, prompted her to think about textual processes in visual, physical ways. Word-processing technology, hypertext, artificial intelligence, and cognitive science are the foundation upon which the CPP-TRS system rests.

"Tonfoni's training as a linguist, her interest in art, and years of research form the background from which she has developed a novel and scientifically validated approach to technical communication. Technical communicators can use the system in a way that is either non-transparent or transparent to the reader of the text. When used non-transparently, technical communicators trained in the system use its tools to structure and organize an ordinary text. The transparent use of the CPP-TRS system leaves visual signs and symbols in the text to document the type and intention of the text so that technical communicators can revise it effectively and efficiently when needed."

1. This paragraph about Technical Writing in CPP-TRS is James Richardson's comment. James Richardson expertly helped me turn my earlier Italian works on CPP-TRS into a shorter English version, which conveys clearly and succinctly my techniques. In order to make my three previously published Italian books on CPP-TRS available quickly to an English audience I have translated each of the single parts which were then expertly edited with the help of James Richardson as technical writer. By explaining the content of my books and how each of the CPP-TRS component actually works, I have been teaching him the basic skills of my system. A both comprehensive and synthetical exposition of his CPP-TRS learning experience may be found in Richardson J., *The Visual Dimension of Writing*, in Intelligent Tutoring Media, Vol. 5, number 2, pp. 86-90, 1994, Intellect, Oxford. This is what I have done many times with my students, some of whom have become trainers themselves, in the sense that they are able to transfer the basic skills of CPP-TRS to newcomers after having acquired them themselves. Some of my students in Italy have also been editing a short introduction to CPP-TRS basic skills. Through an invitation by a colleague, Professor Dr. Rothkegel, at the Fachhochschule Hannover-Germany, I have also trained German students in CPP-TRS basic skills for Technical Writing in 1994, just as I did with James Richardson. I have also trained a group of teachers in Spain (Balearic Islands) in order to get a Spanish project started in 1994. It has always been my intention to transfer knowledge and mastering of CPP-TRS basic skills in different languages. It is part of my CPP-TRS training and of my system to test acquisition by having students report with written texts the content of my teaching. Teaching CPP-TRS basic skills explicitly encourages an active reaction on the student's part as a way to test the learning process. Students are naturally becoming aware of the process made visible through CPP-TRS tools and techniques. All the material, which has been generated as a way to exercise and practice CPP-TRS as well as personal comments about the experience, is available for consultation upon request. Some anthologies of particularly significant exercise texts have also been published.

Visual overview on applications: what has been done and what is being done

All of the following applications are designed by the author, presented as a visual overview of the different fields of application. CPP-TRS and CPP-TRS applications are the intellectual property of Graziella Tonfoni: for further information the reader is welcome to contact her directly.

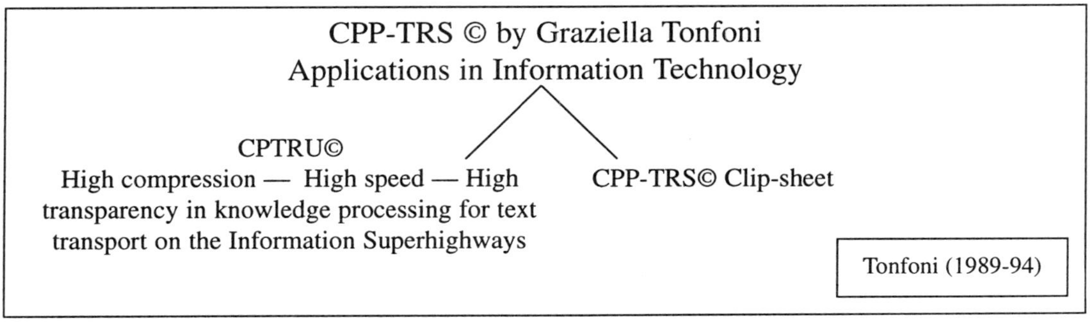

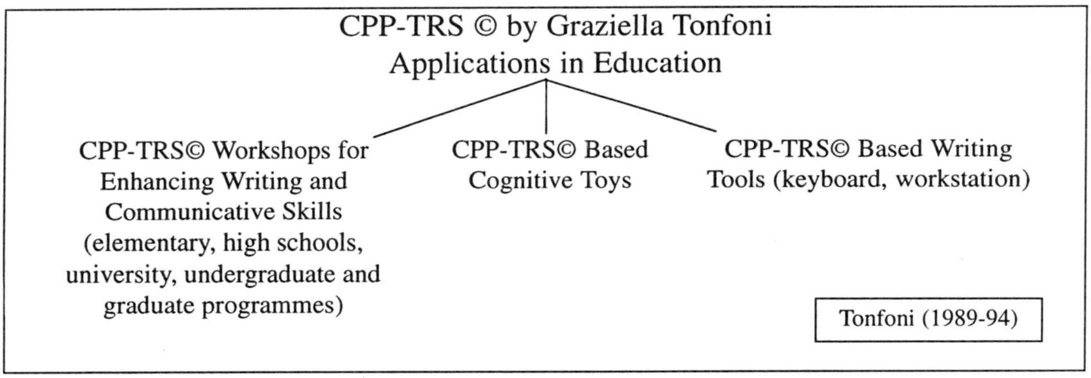

CPP-TRS © by Graziella Tonfoni
Applications in Information Processing

Technical Writing

- Manual revision and technical writing techniques
- Client interviewing and information acquisition
- Information packaging and integration
- Translation support

Corporate Communication Training

- Facilitation and effectiveness of group working sessions and meetings
- Improvement of client presentations
- Internal training

Navigation Tools Production

- E-mail and internal message filtering and delivery
- Enhancement of software interface design and production
- Information filing and retrieval

Tonfoni (1989-94)

CPP-TRS © by Graziella Tonfoni
Applications in Entertainment

CPP-TRS© based special effects in writing book previews

3-D text production and text motion

CPP-TRS© based writing paths and writing trips

CPP-TRS© based writing parks and writing environments

Tonfoni (1989-94)

Author Biography

Graziella Tonfoni was born in Bologna on 23 July 1957. She attended the Liceo Classico Galvani and passed her final exams with 60/60 cum laude in 1976. She was among the top 50 students in Italy and received the Ettore Majorana Certificate in 1975. She received her Ph.D. in Linguistics in 1980 from the University of Bologna, where she now teaches Computational Linguistics and Natural Language Processing, with a dissertation on Generative Grammar Applications to Translation (110/110 cum laude). She is known for her contributions to textual theory, cognitive science, artificial intelligence, communications, training and multimedia education.

Dr Tonfoni has been visiting scholar at the following American universities and research institutes:

— Massachusetts Institute of Technology (at the invitation of Prof. Noam Chomsky and Prof. Marvin Minsky)

— Harvard University (at the invitation of Prof. Susumu Kuno)

— Bolt Beranek and Newman (at the invitation of Dr Bertram Bruce).

In addition, she has given seminars and lectures at Cornell University at the invitation of Prof. Solà), the University of Illinois, Chicago Circle (at the invitation of Prof. Makkai), the University of California at Berkeley (at the invitation of Prof. Fillmore), Stanford Research International (at the invitation of Dr Hobbs), Boston University (at the invitation of Prof. Fraser), the University of Massachusetts at Amherst (at the invitation of Prof. Lehnert), M.I.T. Dept. of Political Sciences (at the invitation of Prof. Alker), the Jet Propulsion Laboratory in Pasadena (at the invitation of Dr Doyle), the Institute for the Learning Sciences (at the invitation of Prof. Schank), Yale University (at the invitation of Prof. Valesio), LJSC NASA, Houston (at the invitation of Dr Culbert), the University of California in San Diego (at the invitation of Prof. Agre) and UCLA (at the invitation of Prof. Smith-Maddox).

Over the last ten years, Dr Tonfoni has developed the CPP-TRS Communicative Positioning Program–Text Representation Systems, on which *Writing as a Visual Art* was based.

The CPP-TRS is an innovative methodology for enhancing the effectiveness of writing, reading and other communication endeavours. Dr Tonfoni uses the CPP-TRS methodology in a writing laboratory that she directs at the University of Bologna. Further, this methodology is used in schools and universities in Italy and elsewhere in Europe. It is also the basis for group-working workshops conducted by Dr Tonfoni for corporations. She has previously been a consultant for Arthur Andersen.

Dr Tonfoni has also personally developed many CPP-TRS applications, some of which are text-processing devices specifically suited to Information Highways, Large Database Navigation and Technical Documentation and Software-Integration Tools.

Dr Tonfoni is the author of 17 books.

She has also published more than 40 scientific articles and she is the author of 10 Technical Reports on Specific Applications of CPP-TRS.

Dr Tonfoni was given the Minerva Award for "Woman in Scientific Research" in Rome in 1984.

Endorsements

Grammar and punctuation show the local structure of a text, but do not clearly indicate the intended rhetorical function of each part, and amateur storytellers often fail in that domain. Tonfoni's system of explicit function symbols could help both language theorists and working writers.

Marvin Minsky

Toshiba Professor of Arts and Sciences, Massachusetts Institute of Technology

This idea, when implemented on a computer, would help to create new writing methods that would help to bring about the computer revolution.

Roger Schank

Director of the Institute for the Learning Sciences, Northwestern University

I think that the whole set of descriptive strategies and techniques that Tonfoni has developed, are very helpful in making explicit, both for teaching and describing, all those different ways a text can be conceived and written (I mean both literary texts and non-literary ones).

Paolo Valesio

Director of the Italian Department, Yale University

References

First I have to acknowledge the *Encyclopedia Britannica*, which has provided the definitions of many of the currently used terms in physics, chemistry and biology.

Similarly, the *Random House Dictionary* has enabled me to check definitions of those terms.

Inconsistencies in the references are due to the different levels of relevance each of the quoted books or articles has when referring to the points made in the present book.

Austin, J.L. (1962), How to do things with words, Oxford, Oxford University Press.

Ballard, D.H., and Brown, C.M. (1982), Computer Vision, New Jersey, Prentice-Hall Inc.

Ballmer, T. (1975), Sprachrekonstruktionssysteme und einige ihrer Anwendingsmöglichkeiten in Satz- und Textlinguistik, Kronenberg, Taunus Schriptor.

Bohr, N. (1922), The Theory of Spectra and Atomic Construction, Cambridge, Cambridge University Press.

— (1934), Atomic Theory and the Description of Nature, Cambridge, Cambridge University Press.

— (1958), Atomic Physics and Human Knowledge, New York, Wiley.

Chomsky, N. (1957), Syntactic Structures, The Hague, Mouton.

— (1965), Aspects of the Theory of Syntax, Cambridge, Mass, MIT Press.

— (1975), The Logical Structure of Linguistic Theory, New York, Plenum Press.

— (1976), Reflections on Language, London, Maurice Temple Smith.

— (1977), Essays on Form and Interpretation, Amsterdam, North Holland Publishing Company.

— (1980), Rules and Representations, Oxford, Blackwell.

Cruttenden, A. (1986), Intonation, Cambridge, Cambridge University Press.

De Beaugrande, R.A. and Dressler, W. (1981), Einführung in die Textlinguistik, Tübingen, Max Niemeyer Verlag.

Eco, U. (1975), Trattato di semiotica, Milano, Bompiani.

Fillmore, C. (1977), "The Case for Case Reported". In Cole, P. and Sadock, J. (eds.), Syntax and Semantics. Volume 8: Grammatical Relations, New York, Academic Press.

— (1980), "The Case for Case". In Bach and Harms (eds.), Universals in Linguistic Theory, 1-88, New York, Holt, Reinhart and Winston.

Geldof, S. (1994), Report on the 1993 Bolzano Int. School in Philosophy and Artificial Intelligence: NLP and Multilinguism. AICOM, 7 (3/4), 227-233.

Ginsberg, K. (1986), Getting from Here to There, Unix Review, January, 45.

Halliday, M.A.K., and Hasan R. (1976), Cohesion in English, Longman.

Hobbs, J.R. (1979), "Coherence and Coreference", in Cognitive Science, 3, 67-90.

Hovy, E., and Nirenburg S. (1992), "Approximating and interlingua in a principled way", in Proceedings of the DARPA Speech and Natural Language Workshop, Nawsthorne.

Joshi, A..K. (1991), "Natural Language Processing", in Science, 253, 1242-1249.

Lehnert, W.G. (1981), "Plot Units and Narrative Summarization", in Cognitive Science, 2, 293-331.

McKevitt, P. (1994a), "Visions for Language", in Proceedings of the Workshop on Integration of Natural Language and Vision Processing. Twelfth American National Conference on Artificial Intelligence (AAAI-94), Seattle, Washington, USA, August, 47-57.

— (ed.) (1994b), Proceedings of the Workshop on Integration of Natural Language and Vision Processing. Twelfth American National Conference on Artificial Intelligence (AAAI-94), Seattle, Washington, USA, August.

— (ed.) (1994c), "Special Issue on Integration of Natural Language and Vision Processing", in Artificial Intelligence Review, 8 (2-3), Dordrecht, Kluwer Academic Publishers.

— (ed.) (1994d), "Integration of Natural Language and Vision Processing: More Computational Models and Systems", in Artificial Intelligence Review, vol. 8, n. 5-6, Dordrecht, Kluwer Academic Publishers.

McQuillan, J.M., and Waldens, D.C. (1977), "The ARPA Network Design Decisions", Computer Networks, 243-289.

Mann, W.C., and Thompson, S.A. (1987), "Rethorical Structure Theory: A Theory of Text Organization", in Polany L. (ed.), The Structure of Discourse, Ablex Publishing Corporation.

Marr, D. (1982), Vision, New York, W.H. Freeman and Company.

Mealing, S., and Yazdani, M. (1990), "A Computer-based iconic language", in Intelligent Tutoring Media, 1 (3), 133-136.

Minsky, M. (1986), The Society of Mind, New York, Simon and Schuster.

— (1975), "A Framework for Representing Knowledge", in Winston P.H. (ed.), The Psychology of Computer Vision, New York, McGraw-Hill, 211-277.

Ó Nualláin, S., and Smith, A.G. (1994), "An Investigation into the Common Semantics of Language and Vision", in The Artificial Intelligence Review, 8, 113-122, Dordrecht, Kluwer Academic Publishers.

Partridge, C. (1986), "Mail Routing Using Domain Names: An Informal Tour", in Proceedings of the 1986 Summer USENIX Conference, 366-76, Usenix Association, Berkeley, Ca.

— (1988), Innovations in Internetworking, Norwood, Ma., Arch House.

Previati, G. (1990), La tecnica della pittura, Milano, Sugarco.

Radford, A. (1988), Transformational Grammar, Cambridge, Cambridge University Press.

Random House Dictionary.

Schank, R.C. (1972), Conceptual Dependency: "A Theory of Natural Language Understanding", Cognitive Psychology, 3(4), 552-631.

— (1981), Inside Computer Understanding, Hillsdale, N.J., Lawrence Erlbaum Ass.

— (1988), The Creative Attitude, New York, Macmillan.

Schank, R.C., and Abelson, R.P. (1977), Scripts, Plans, Goals and Understanding: An Inquiry into Human Knowledge Structures, Hillsdale, N.J., Lawrence Erlbaum Associates.

Searle, J. (1968), Speech Acts: An Essay in the Philosophy of Language, Cambridge, Cambridge University Press.

Sebeok, T.A. (ed.) (1960), Style in Language, Cambridge, MIT Press.

Shu, N.C. (1988), Visual Programming, New York, Van Nostrand Reinhold Company.

Srihari, R.K. (1994), "Computational models for integrating linguistic and visual information: a survey", in The Artificial Intelligence Review, 8, 349-369, Dordrecht, Kluwer Academic Publishers.

Tannenbaum, A.S. (1987), Computer Networks, Englewood Cliffs, N.J., Prentice Hall.

Tonfoni, G. (1988) "Percezione concettuale del testo e processo direzionali di riassunto" (Text conceptual perception and summarization goal-oriented processes), in Atti del Diciannovesimo Congresso Internazionale della Società Linguistica Italiana su "Dalla parte del ricevente: percezione, comprensione, interpretazione, 8-10 novembre 1985, Roma,edited by T. De Mauro, S. Gensini, M.E. Piemontese, 253-259, Roma, Bulzoni

— (1990), Text Representation Systems, Helsinki, Nobili, Pesaro, Italy and Eurographica Oy, Helskinky, Finland.

— (1990), La lettura strategica. Tecniche cognitive per leggere di più e meglio (Strategic Readign. Cognitive Techniques to Read More and Better), with G. Tassi (technical writer), Milano, Mondadori Informatica.

— (1991), La scrittura multimediale: Tecniche di progettazione e design testuale (Multimedia Writing: Textual Design and Architecturing), Treviso, Pagus.

— (1991), La comunicazione aziendale come arte visiva (Business Communication as Visual Art), Treviso, Pagus.

— (1991), Didattica del testo. Curricolo di formazione linguistica per gli insegnanti (Teaching through Texts. The Teacher's Guide to Text Writing and Reading), Teramo, Giunti e Lisciani.

— (1991), Sistemi cognitivi complessi (Complex Cognitive Systems), Treviso, Pagus.

— (1991), "Communicative cooperative interaction models: gapfilling processes by reformulation" in Referate der Dritten Arbeitstagung Dialoganalyse III, 1990, Bologna, edited by S. Stati, E. Weigand, F. Hundsnurscher, 405-414, Tubingen, Max Niemeyer Verlag.

— (1991), "Traduzione e sistemi di rappresentazione della conoscenza" (Translation and knowledge representation systems), in Koinè, Annali della Scuola Normale Superiore per Interpreti e Traduttori, 17 aprile 1991, San Pellegrino, 1, (2), 33-56, Misano, aprile.

— (1991), "Linguaggio come arte visiva. Sistemi di rappresentazione del testo" (Language and Visual art. Text Representation Systems), in Atti del XII Festival International de la Video et des Artes Electroniques — Tavola Rotonda, settembre 1991, Locarno.

— (1992), Partitura, solfeggio, movimento: Note di esecuzione di scrittura (Partitura, Sol-fa, Movement: Notes on Execution of Writing), Treviso, Pagus.

— (1992), "Traduzione e scienze cognitive: sistemi di rappresentazione del testo" (Translation and cognitive sciences: text representation systems), in Atti della Fiera Internazionale della Traduzione, 10-12 dicembre 1990, Riccione, 57-73, Forlì, Ateneo Editrice.

— (1992), "Processi di autoriflessione cognitiva ed apprendimento. Laboratorio di multimedialità attiva e tecniche di visualizzazione dei percorsi di traduzione dei testi" (Cognitive self-reflection processes and learning. Active multimedia laboratory and visualization techniques of text translation processes), in Atti del Convegno su "Il computer nell'apprendimento e nell'autoapprendimento linguistico", 11-12 ottobre 1991, Bologna, edited by R. Rossini Favretti, 77-84, Bologna, Monduzzi.

— (1992), "Cognitive training and teaching support systems in artificial intelligence: on language and reasoning", in Settentrione, 3, 22-29, Università di Turku, Turku, Finland.

— (1992), "Dalla rappresentazione della conoscenza alla 'scienza della conoscenza': sistemi di rappresentazione del testo" (From knowledge representation to 'knowledge science': text representation systems), in Calcolatori e scienze umane. Archeologia e arte, scienze giuridiche e sociali, linguistica, letteratura. Scritti del convegno organizzato dall'Accademia Nazionale dei Lincei e dalla Fondazione IBM Italia, 315-328, Milano, Etaslibri.

— (1992), "Intelligenza artificiale: da un modello comunicativo 'chiuso' ad un sistema 'aperto' di gestione e revisione dell'implicito nelle conversazioni a scopo collaborativo" (Artificial intelligence: from a 'closed' communicative model to an 'open' system for managing and revising 'implicit knowledge' in cooperative conversation), in La Linguistica Pragmatica. Atti del XXIV Congresso, 415-429, Roma, Bulzoni.

— (1992), "Modelli di rappresentazione lessicale per un ambiente multimediale" (Lexical representation models for a multimedia environment), in Atti del Seminario Internazionale di Studi sul Lessico, 2-5 aprile 1992, Forlì-San Marino, Bologna, Clueb.

— (1992), "La multimedialità attiva" (Active multimedia), in Media Duemila, X, (4), 24-33, April.

— (1992), "E il lettore diventa scrittore" (The reader becomes the writer), in Media Duemila, X, (7), 67-73, July-August.

— (1993), "Applicazioni della metodologia CPP-TRS in ambiente didattico" (Applications of CPP-TRS methodology to a teaching environment), in Informatica & Scuola, 2, 26-29, January.

— (1993), "Produrre multimedialità" (Multimedia production), in Media Duemila, XI, (2), 27-29, March.

— (1993), "Il disegno multimediale" (Multimedia drawing), in Media Duemila, XI, (4), 78-80, April.

— (1994), "CPP-TRS: on Using Visual Cognitive Symbols to Enhance Communication Effectiveness", ISMCR-94: Topical Workshop on Virtual Reality, Proceedings of the Fourth International Symposium on Measurement and Control in Robotics, 136-142, NASA, Houston, Usa, Nov. 30-Dec. 3; Library of Congress #94-69310.

— (1994), Writing as a Visual Art, Oxford, Intellect (with J. Richardson and with a Foreword by Marvin Minsky), now being translated into Japanese.

— (1994), Frammenti testuali (Textual Fragments), Parma, Zara.

— (1994), "La metodologia CPP-TRS per l'interazione uomo-macchina" (The CPP-TRS methdology for man-machine interaction), in AEI — Automazione Energia Informazione, 81, (6), 69-74, June.

— (1994), "A dynamic model for representing invisible aspects of language", in Atti del IV Convegno dell'Associazione Italiana per l'Intelligenza Artificiale, Atti del gruppo di lavoro su "Aspetti Epistemologici e Gnoseologici dell'Intelligenza Artificiale, 26-28 settembre, edited by M. Somalvico, 47-50, Università di Parma, Parma.

— (1995), Abitare il Testo (Living in Text), Treviso, Pagus.

Van Dijk, T. (1969), "Sémantique structurale et analyse thématique", Lingua, 23, 28-53.

Wilensky, R. (1983), Planning and Understanding, Reading, Addison Wesley.

Winston, P.H. (1992), Artificial Intelligence, Reading, Addison Wesley.

Communication Patterns and Textual Forms

Graziella Tonfoni

intellect™

First Published in 1996 by
Intellect Books
EFAE, Earl Richards Road North, Exeter EX2 6AS

Consulting editor: Masoud Yazdani
Copy Editor: Wendi Momen
Production: Robin Beecroft

A catalogue record for this book is available from the British Library

ISBN 1-871516-65-X

Printed and bound in Great Britain by Cromwell Press, Wiltshire